The One-Pot
PALEO
Cookbook

The One-Pot
PALEO
Cookbook

100+ Effortless Meals for Your Slow Cooker, Skillet, Sheet Pan, and More

Shelby Law Ruttan

ROCKRIDGE
PRESS

Interior and Cover Designer: Jill Lee
Art Producer: Karen Williams
Editor: Carolyn Abate
Production Editor: Andrew Yackira

Photography © Evi Abeler, Food styling by Albane Sharrard, pp. viii, x, 18, 20, 42, 88, 104, 130; © Jennifer Davick p. ii; © Nadine Greef, pp 68, 160.

Author photo courtesy of © Lana Ortiz Photography.

ISBN: Print 978-1-64152-759-0 | eBook 978-1-64152-760-6

R0

*To Phillip, a.k.a. Grumpy, who encourages me to
achieve my goals and told me a long time ago
I should be writing a cookbook.*

CONTENTS

INTRODUCTION

I spent most of my adult life on the other side of 200—on the scale, that is. Once I had given birth to my two children, the weight did not fall off as easily as I had put it on during pregnancy. I spent the majority of my children's time at home as the overweight mom. Then, in 2006, after my weight skyrocketed to 264 pounds, I opted for weight-loss surgery. I did great for the first five years, then the honeymoon was over.

Even though I couldn't eat a lot of food in one sitting, I hadn't really changed my habits. Processed foods continued to be a part of my daily life, and I was on the upward path on the scale yet again. I developed vitamin deficiencies, partly due to the surgery I had and partly due to a lack of the right kind of foods in my diet.

By October 2017 I changed my diet. I needed to get back to healthier eating and my husband was now dealing with pre-diabetes. Thanks to the Paleo diet, I've been able to maintain a healthy weight, but getting here involved another journey. We initially started following the Keto diet. But I quickly realized we were also following many of the Paleo guidelines.

Our lifestyle allows our diets to be very close to the way cave dwellers lived and ate. In a way, we eat like hunters and homesteaders. We consume a lot of game meat due to our hunting activities and always have plenty of garden produce on hand. It's no wonder that Paleo became even more interesting to me. By following Paleo a little more than Keto when it came to fruits and vegetables, we were able to bring the variety from the garden back into our meal plan.

Part of our success with this plan was understanding the food we were eating. I researched what foods we could eat and learned how to prepare them. I started creating recipes with short prep times, minimal ingredients, all cooked in one pot. This freed up my time tremendously, and we felt better in the process. A busy lifestyle will no longer be the reason you can't follow the Paleo diet. It is my hope that these recipes will encourage you to stick to the diet and not fall back into your old ways of eating. Think of this cookbook as a tool to help you succeed.

Chapter One
PALEO, THE ONE-POT WAY

Following the Paleo diet can be challenging, to say the least. Whether you are eating dinner out or cooking at home, sticking to the diet can feel overwhelming.

With our busy lives, having recipes on hand that are quick to prepare, delicious, and nutritious all at the same time is another challenge. Most of us don't have the time to spend 30 minutes preparing ingredients, not to mention the time it takes to cook those ingredients. This is why I wrote this book—to share the basics of what's needed to start creating delicious meals with a prep time of 15 minutes or less. To make it even easier, these meals are made in one pot. So, you not only have quick prep time but also quick cleanup afterward!

Paleo Basics

The Paleo diet is based on the idea of eating the way our prehistoric ancestors ate during the Paleolithic period when humans lived in caves and roamed the earth as hunters and gatherers, and a time when it is believed that farming didn't exist.

Based on this assumption, grains, legumes, and dairy products are **not included** in the Paleo diet. The one exception regarding legumes is green beans, which are a nutrient-dense food. And, the exception among dairy products is ghee, which is clarified butter with the milk solids removed. Nut flours can be used in place of flours made from grain.

Any plants consumed would also be in their natural state, as they were harvested. These so-called "cavemen" are assumed to have lived off the land consuming animal protein, eggs, fruits, vegetables, nuts, and seeds. The animals that were consumed lived off the land, too, eating a grass-fed diet. It's fair to say this was organic, in the most general sense, because the animals were not fed nor raised by humans for consumption.

Embracing a Paleo diet, in today's world, is really about eating natural, whole, and organic as much as possible. Following in these cave ancestors' footsteps requires removing processed foods from our diets, while adding whole foods to replace them. And although that may sound daunting to some, I promise the payoff—in terms of your improved health—is worth it.

HEALTH BENEFITS

People follow the Paleo diet for a variety of reasons—the most common being better health. The main idea of this diet is to eat unprocessed foods. That means no added preservatives, artificial flavorings, or other food additives. Basically, if it is in a box or can, it is likely processed. By eliminating processed foods from your diet, you may reap several benefits, including reduced risk for diabetes, high blood sugar, heart disease, and inflammation. Direct health benefits of a Paleo diet include:

Healthy heart: The Paleo diet is loaded with foods considered excellent for promoting a healthy heart and reducing the risk of heart disease. Foods such as avocados, leafy greens, nuts, and seeds can contribute to your heart health and are commonly eaten on the Paleo diet.

Improved digestion: If you are gluten or dairy intolerant, following the Paleo diet will offer some symptom relief by eliminating the ingredients you are sensitive to that can cause digestive issues such as bloating, constipation, and diarrhea.

Reduced inflammation: If an autoimmune condition, such as irritable bowel syndrome, lupus, or Hashimoto's disease is present, following the Paleo diet may help lessen symptoms and heal the body.

Weight loss: Removing processed foods from the diet reduces the number of carbohydrates consumed. Therefore, if you need to lose weight, following the Paleo diet may help. As a result, you may gain overall better health from the elimination of foods that damage your system, making you feel better.

WHAT TO EAT

The Paleo diet is based on eating only foods available during the Paleolithic period. But we don't live during that time, so it's important to follow this way of eating through the lens of our modern times.

Fresh fruit and vegetables: Organically grown is preferred. Fruits, vegetables, and tubers are allowed. Choose the lower-carb fruit over the higher-carb option if you are looking to keep carbohydrates low. Tubers, such as sweet potatoes, are high in vitamin A, making them a better choice than the white potato. Dark leafy greens, such as spinach, arugula, and kale, and other vegetables such as cauliflower, broccoli, and cabbage, are all nutrient-dense choices. All fruits are allowed; however, berries are a great choice and lower in carbohydrates than other fruits.

Minimal alcohol: Drinking in moderation is considered okay. Distilled liquors are in; fermented alcohol is out. This means no beer. Brandy, gin, rum, tequila, whiskey, and vodka are allowed, as they are distilled. Red wine, although it is fermented alcohol, is high in antioxidants and allowed.

Nuts, seeds, and oils: All nuts (*with the exception of peanuts*, which are considered a legume) are allowed, including almonds, pecans, walnuts, sunflower seeds, pumpkin seeds, and more. Coconut oil, avocado oil, and olive oil are the three most common oils used on this diet. Avoid vegetable oil and hydrogenated oils.

Protein from the land: Consume grass-fed meats, such as beef, pork, chicken, turkey, and lamb. Wild game, such as venison, bison, elk, rabbit, boar, and pheasant, is also great, if available. Eggs are another excellent source of protein.

Protein from the sea: Wild-caught fish is preferred—if possible. Salmon is an excellent source of omega-3 fatty acids as well as vitamin D and is low on the mercury scale. Other fish to enjoy are haddock, cod, halibut, shrimp, and other shellfish. Tuna is okay but is high on the mercury scale and should be consumed in moderation.

Other Paleo-approved foods: Some other foods that weren't around during Paleo times are also considered okay on the Paleo diet. Ghee is a highly clarified butter that has had its milk solids removed and it is approved for Paleo dieters. Maple syrup and raw honey are allowed, as they are considered unprocessed sweeteners in their natural state. Coffee, though it likely did not exist as a beverage then, is also acceptable due to the fact that there can be benefits to drinking it. Drinking coffee black, unsweetened, or with coconut oil or ghee is considered the best way to gain the most benefits from coffee.

The following is a handy one-sheet guideline for the Paleo diet.

FOOD TO ENJOY VERSUS FOODS TO AVOID

ENJOY	MODERATION	AVOID

ORGANIC, GRASS-FED MEAT
- Beef
- Bison
- Chicken
- Lamb
- Pork
- Turkey
- Venison

EGGS

FISH AND SHELLFISH
- Cod
- Crab
- Halibut
- Oysters
- Salmon
- Scallops
- Shrimp
- Snapper
- Tuna

VEGETABLES
- Artichoke
- Asparagus
- Bell peppers
- Bok choy
- Broccoli
- Brussels sprouts
- Cabbage
- Carrots
- Cauliflower
- Cucumber
- Green beans
- Leafy greens
- Mushrooms
- Onions
- Sweet potatoes
- Tomatoes
- Winter squash
- Zucchini

FRUITS
- Apples
- Bananas
- Blackberries
- Blueberries
- Kiwi
- Lemon
- Lime
- Mango
- Oranges
- Peach
- Pear
- Raspberries
- Strawberries

NUTS AND SEEDS
- Almond
- Cashew
- Chia seeds
- Flaxseed
- Hazelnut
- Hemp seed
- Macadamia
- Pecan
- Pine nut
- Pumpkin seeds
- Sesame seeds
- Sunflower seeds
- Walnut

HEALTHY FATS AND OILS
- Avocado oil
- Coconut oil
- Duck fat
- Ghee
- Nut and seed butters
- Olive oil

SWEETENERS
- Erythritol
- Honey
- Maple syrup
- Stevia

ALL GRAINS
- Barley
- Corn
- Oats
- Rye
- Wheat

ALL DAIRY EXCEPT GHEE

LEGUMES
- Black beans
- Black-eyed peas
- Cannellini beans
- Kidney beans
- Lentils
- Peanuts
- Soybeans

REFINED VEGETABLE OILS
- Canola
- Margarine
- Peanut
- Sunflower

PROCESSED FOODS
- Artificial sweeteners
- Baked goods
- Candy bars
- Fruit juice
- Packaged meals
- Sugary snacks and treats

THE PALEO KETO CONVERSION

The Paleo and Keto diets are actually quite close in terms of their guidelines. Both diets encourage grass-fed animal products, saturated fats, and oils as well as a low-carb lifestyle. Both are low-carb diets that eliminate grains, sugars, and legumes.

Paleo allows you to eat a little more carbohydrate but it eliminates dairy. It is assumed that the cavemen did not milk cattle. Many people who follow Paleo do so because they have an intolerance to certain foods, such as lactose in milk.

Keto allows dairy products, but milk is avoided. Milk is higher in carbohydrates, so coconut milk or nut milk is normally substituted. Although dairy is not restricted in a Keto diet, it is higher in calories and, if you're doing Keto to lose weight, overdoing dairy might become a factor in a weight-loss stall. Many Keto bread and biscuit recipes incorporate cheese into the ingredients. Many recipes that are Keto can also be Paleo with a few substitutions.

People follow each diet for different reasons. Some follow it for weight loss, whereas others adhere to the diets for health reasons. People with diabetes may look to these diets as something to help them get control of their blood sugar levels.

Tracking macronutrients is very common for both Paleo and Keto followers. Because each individual has their own set scale of macronutrients to follow, a percentage of each macronutrient is included for each recipe in this cookbook.

Paleo Made Easy

When it comes to following the Paleo diet, it doesn't have to be hard. The goal of this cookbook is to help you overcome the obstacles you may encounter when preparing to cook your meals and to help you succeed by sharing with you how to plan ahead. You will learn how to be prepared before you cook your meals as well as pick up some meal prep tips along the way. Recipes can be prepped in 15 minutes or less, making cooking easier and more enjoyable. And making your meals all in one pot makes it even easier, with less mess to clean up and fewer dishes to wash.

Each recipe in this cookbook has taken into account the amount of ingredient prep time as well as the amount of work you will have to do while cooking your meal. This process has been designed to be as easy as possible for you to achieve Paleo cooking success. There are tips on how to prepare your ingredients as well as the process to follow when cooking your meals.

THE WONDERS OF ONE POT

One-pot cooking is a fuss-free way to prepare dinner. It is a meal full of wonderful aromas and flavors that stimulate the senses and satisfy your hunger. And, for a busy parent, it's really a saving grace. Cooking in one pot is not only time-saving, but it produces a flavorful meal and leaves you with the easiest cleanup afterward.

When many people think of one-pot cooking, they think of comfort food—warm, inviting, all cozy in one pot. All a one-pot meal needs is a spoon to dig straight into the pot, transferring the meal to your plate.

The recipes in this cookbook are made to suit everyone in your family, no matter what diet they follow. The recipes are made with familiar easy-to-find ingredients, some of which you likely already have in your kitchen. These delicious Paleo one-pot recipes will make your life easier and satisfy your hunger with very little effort. This method of cooking is about to become your favorite way to make dinner for your family!

SUPER SIMPLE INGREDIENTS

Ingredients used in these recipes are common kitchen ingredients and are not hard to find. There are plenty of fresh vegetables worked into these meals without a lot of other ingredients. Adding too many flavors to the pot can ruin the delicious flavor of the very food you are trying to highlight.

Many ingredients can be prepped ahead, or, for convenience, purchased already prepared. Although some people don't mind making their own veggie noodles, it is very common to see this item in the store already prepped. You should also be able to easily find precut or shredded vegetables, such as zucchini, butternut squash, mushrooms, celery, carrots, and onions, to name a few.

FUSS-FREE PREP

A one-pot recipe can be delicious, but if it has 15 or more ingredients and requires more than 30 minutes of prep time, it is not going to help your busy life. The one-pot recipes in this cookbook were created to solve the problem of long prep times by using fewer ingredients. Nearly all recipes call for 10 ingredients—some have less and some have more. And we aren't counting the basics, like olive oil, salt, and pepper. The prep time has been simplified with tips to make it easier to have your ingredients ready in just 15 minutes.

Not everyone has time to create three different dishes every night. One-pot cooking brings those three dishes together, making mealtime easier for the cook. Using this cookbook as a guide, you can create delicious meals that fit the Paleo diet—all in one pot.

These recipes will deliver what a one-pot meal implies—fast prep, delicious results, and easy cleanup. The shortcuts provided give you the option of an even faster prep time as well as other cooking options for your one-pot wonder meals.

PALEO PREP TIPS

When preparing the ingredients for a recipe, there are a few tips to keep in mind to simplify the process. Whether it is a kitchen tool or the option to find an already prepped ingredient, there is always more than one way to achieve the goal.

* **Prep and portion fresh vegetables ahead of time.** Preparing the vegetables for your recipes ahead of time is key. Taking the time to clean and prepare the fresh vegetables after you get home from shopping can make your entire week easier. Once the vegetables have been cleaned and prepared in the way needed for a recipe, put them into an airtight container and label the container with the recipe they will be used for.

* **Precut fruits and vegetables.** Buying prepared vegetables for your meals is another time-saving option. Many grocery stores now offer prepackaged containers of zucchini noodles, spiralized sweet potatoes, and even the holy trinity of chopped onion, bell pepper, and celery.

* **Keep a well-stocked pantry.** Keep pantry staples, such as canned coconut milk, frequently used spices (garlic and onion powder, dried basil, oregano, and thyme), coconut aminos, fish sauce, and beef and chicken broth on hand. This ensures you have them at the ready at all times.

* **Nuts and seeds.** Nuts and seeds are extremely common in Paleo cooking. Buy chopped nuts in bulk so it is easy to add just what you need without doing the chopping yourself.

* **Precooking.** There are foods you can cook ahead to save time. Foods such as bacon can be partially cooked and then frozen or refrigerated until needed. You can also roast a chicken or turkey, make a meal of it, and then portion out the amount you may need for a recipe that calls for cooked chicken. The same goes for any roasts you make.

The Paleo Kitchen

To make tasty food in the Paleo kitchen, you need to have the right tools and ingredients, as well as the right mind-set. Be prepared to discover new ingredients and combinations of foods to enjoy in ways you may not have thought possible when following Paleo. You may be surprised that you won't need many, if any, unfamiliar ingredients in your kitchen.

At the most, you may need to buy three or four new ingredients. Ever heard of arrowroot powder? Maybe, maybe not. But rest assured, as you continue to live the Paleo lifestyle, this and other "newer" ingredients will not go to waste. You will see these ingredients show up often in the recipes in this cookbook.

PANTRY ESSENTIALS

Each item in the following list is an ingredient used in several recipes in this cookbook. You should stock your pantry with these items to have on hand and ready when needed.

Almond butter. Necessary for making some Thai-style sauces and it can also be an added topping to the grain-free cereal, if desired.

Almond meal. Essential for a grain-free cereal and it can also be used to add a coating to fried meat or a crumbly texture to a topping, such as for fish.

Arrowroot powder. This works very much like cornstarch and is used to thicken sauces.

Chicken and beef broth. Many soups and sauces will use either chicken or beef broth as an ingredient. Having a couple containers of each type on hand is a good idea.

Coconut aminos. Used in place of soy sauce, coconut aminos, though with a sweeter, less fermented taste, is a good substitute for soy.

Coconut milk and coconut cream. These two items are probably the most essential ingredients in your Paleo kitchen and are used in many recipes in this cookbook. You should keep at least two cans of each on hand, as you may go through this ingredient quickly.

Cooking oil. Coconut, olive, or avocado oil work in any recipes that call for oil. The oil is primarily used for sautéing and frying.

Diced canned tomatoes. There are several soup and stew recipes that use canned diced tomatoes.

Fish sauce. Although not used extensively, this pantry item is necessary for that umami flavor you want in soups and sauces.

Ghee. Also called clarified butter, ghee is made by removing the milk solids from butter. Ghee is used as an ingredient to sauté vegetables and add flavor in several recipes in this book.

PERISHABLE ESSENTIALS

Perishable ingredients used often in this cookbook are listed here. Some must be kept in the refrigerator or freezer, whereas others require storage in a cool, dry area.

Avocado. Filled with good fat and high fiber, avocados are one of the most loved ingredients on the Paleo diet. They can be incorporated into recipes or used on the side.

Beef, fish, pork, poultry, and seafood. These items have a short shelf life if refrigerated. They must be refrigerated until ready to use and can easily be portioned and frozen for long-term storage if bought in bulk.

Bell peppers. Bell peppers should be kept refrigerated to prolong their shelf life. They are great for stuffing, roasting, and adding to stir-fries and they provide color and texture to your meal.

Butternut squash. This versatile squash is used in stews, soups, stir-fries, curries, and more! Whole butternut squash, although perishable, will store for a longer time if kept in a cool, dry spot.

Cauliflower. This ingredient stands in for rice in many dishes and is the main ingredient in several others. Cauliflower rice is the whole cauliflower chopped into small pieces that resemble rice. It can be stir-fried, microwaved, or steamed. Refrigerator storage is recommended for this ingredient.

Eggs. These should be kept refrigerated until you are ready to use them.

Fresh herbs. Fresh basil, cilantro, thyme, and sage are used throughout this cookbook. Store them with the stems wrapped in a damp paper towel, then refrigerate in a storage bag.

Garlic. This ingredient is a staple for adding flavor to food. A little can go a long way. Its shelf life is a little longer than some other perishables.

Onions. Another way to boost flavor in your recipes is with onions. You'll find many recipes in this book that use onion in some form or another.

Zucchini. Used raw or cooked; it is often used as a pasta substitute.

PALEO IN A PINCH

At some point, you might find you don't have the time or an ingredient to make a meal. When this happens, it is a good idea to have a formula so you can bring together a meal in a pinch. This formula can help you combine ingredients to stay Paleo and resist the temptation to stray from the diet.

As you get further into the Paleo diet and become more familiar with how it works, you, too, can come up with your own ideas on how to put one-pot meals together. This simple basic formula is one you can follow to achieve your own delicious creations!

Keeping a few basic Paleo-approved foods around will help you stay on track and make it easier for you to enjoy a stress-free meal. The idea is to choose a vegetable, protein, and sauce from the list following. Combine these items to create a meal that will give you the nutrients your body needs along with the flavor and satisfaction you crave.

Choose a Vegetable

- Broccoli, chopped or in florets
- Cabbage Noodles (page 78)
- Cauliflower rice
- Leafy greens, such as spinach or kale
- Zucchini noodles, or other veggie noodles

Choose a Protein

- Chicken thighs or drumsticks
- Eggs
- Ground beef or pork
- Precooked bacon
- Shrimp, or other seafood

Choose a Sauce

- Alfredo sauce, dairy-free
- Guacamole
- Low-carb nut sauce (similar to peanut sauce, made with a nut butter, like almond butter)
- Marinara or Bolognese sauce
- Salsa

One-Pot Equipment and Tools

There is nothing more tiring than spending a lot of time in the kitchen, on your feet, preparing ingredients and cooking the meal, only to have a huge mess to clean up afterward. It's not only tiring but also a bit depressing when you see the mess! After cooking and eating dinner, who wants to spend another 30 minutes or more just cleaning up?

One-pot meals are the solution to this problem that I just love. Once the ingredients are prepped and the meal is in the pot, I can clean up from prep and wait for dinner to be ready. After dinner, the mess is minimal and cleanup time is short. The equipment listed here is about to become your best friend when making the recipes in this cookbook.

 Casserole or baking dish: All the meal's components are combined here and then baked in the oven and served in the same dish. I consider a baking dish to be an oblong or round casserole, or a muffin pan.

 **Cast iron skillet:** This very versatile cooking device can be used on the stovetop or in the oven. It holds heat and distributes it evenly, making it ideal for one-pot cooking. All recipes that use a cast iron skillet in this cookbook should be at least 12 inches in diameter.

 Large skillet: This usually refers to one a bit larger than 12 inches in size. There are regular skillets and nonstick skillets, which are referred to in each recipe. Other skillet sizes are mentioned when a recipe calls for it.

 Mixing bowls: Although it is ideal to mix and cook everything in the same dish, it may not always be possible. For example, recipes for casseroles and muffins usually require a mixing bowl (or two) in which to combine the ingredients before cooking. I still consider the recipe to be a one-pot meal, as long as the entire meal is baked in one pot or pan.

Sheet pan: This is, basically, an oversize rimmed baking sheet on which your entire meal is laid out and roasted. It can be lined with parchment paper or aluminum foil for even easier cleanup.

Slow cooker or Instant Pot, or other electric pressure cooker: These can be used interchangeably and there will be instructions on how to use the slow cooker should you not own an electric pressure cooker, and vice versa.

Stockpot and Dutch oven: Ideal for making soups, stews, and roasts. You can start and finish on the stove or, if making a roast, move it to the oven to finish cooking.

OTHER MUST-HAVES

There are a few kitchen items essential to have on hand for preparing the recipes in this cookbook. These must-have items are very common, and you probably have most of them in your kitchen.

Chef's knife. Whether you are chopping vegetables or cutting meat, a good set of knives is something every kitchen needs. Most important is a chef's knife for cutting vegetables and doing meat prep and a paring knife for small tasks such as cutting fruit and small vegetables.

Cutting boards. It is highly recommended to have two cutting boards, if possible. One (preferably a nonporous cutting board) dedicated to meats, and another for vegetables. A dishwasher-safe board that is also nonslip is a good choice.

Measuring cups and spoons. When measuring ingredients, both dry and liquid measuring cups are necessary. A set of measuring spoons is also needed to portion out herbs, spices, and seasonings.

Meat thermometer. This is the best way to gauge the internal temperature of cooked meat and be sure your roasts, steaks, chicken, and pork are cooked properly.

Vegetable peeler. This tool is needed to remove the outer skin of butternut squash, carrots, sweet potatoes, and more.

A FEW NICE-TO-HAVES

It is nice to have some tools in the kitchen that make life a little easier. Anything that makes meal prep faster and more convenient is a huge plus. Following are just a few of my favorite kitchen tools that are nice to have.

Food processor. A food processor saves a lot of time in the kitchen. It will turn your cauliflower into rice in seconds. It also will shred, dice, and purée fruits and other vegetables.

Garlic peeler. This tool makes fast work of removing garlic skins from cloves.

Garlic press. You can probably live without this tool, but it sure is nice to have! A garlic press saves you from the tedious task of hand-chopping those tiny cloves.

Kitchen scale. This is handy to have in the kitchen and works great for weighing and portioning meats you buy in bulk.

Spiralizer. A spiralizer will make your life easier when doing meal prep. It is a fairly inexpensive kitchen tool that I highly recommend for a Paleo kitchen. It saves time preparing vegetables, and you can do the prep ahead and refrigerate the vegetables until you're ready for them.

SLOW COOKER AND INSTANT POT

Although the slow cooker has been on the home cooking scene for years now, the Instant Pot, also known as an electric pressure cooker, is a newer sensation in the world of home cooks. Both cooking methods are easy and make delicious one-pot meals.

The slow cooker will cook meals in one pot over a long period, usually from 4 to 8 hours. It is an insulated ceramic crock surrounded by a heating unit, maintaining a steady low temperature to cook the food. Some slow cookers have removable pots, making them even easier to clean. The low and slow cooking process produces very tender meats and blends flavors nicely.

The Instant Pot cooks food at higher temperatures, sealed and under pressure. The cool thing about this cooking method is that it reduces your cooking time drastically while, at the same time, infusing flavors and retaining vitamins and nutrients. The Instant Pot offers several settings from sauté to simmer and slow cook. The inner pot is removable and easy to clean, which is another big plus for a busy cook.

Both the slow cooker and Instant Pot are excellent for one-pot meals. Depending on your situation, one may be better for you than the other.

Sesame Chicken, page 122

About These Recipes

The Paleo diet is not as difficult of a lifestyle as it may seem. The purpose of this cookbook is to assist those who want to follow Paleo and don't want to spend a lot of time in the kitchen. You can produce delicious home-cooked meals for your family with minimal cleanup required and still have time to relax or do other things afterward.

Easy Paleo prepared in one pan: Whether it's a skillet, sheet pan, or slow cooker. All recipes in this book are cooked in one cooking vessel and are easy to prepare!

Approximately 10 ingredients: Yes, you can prepare a delicious and flavorful meal in just one pot with minimal ingredients! The recipes in this cookbook use about 10 ingredients—some less, some more—not counting salt, pepper, and olive oil.

Prep times around 15 minutes: The time to put your meal together has been streamlined. With the tips included in this cookbook, your prep time will be no more than 15 minutes.

Recipe icons that indicate the cooking vessel: Each recipe is labeled with an icon to indicate the cooking method.

Recipe labels: All recipes in this cookbook follow the Paleo diet guidelines. If a recipe is dairy-free (dairy is only included in the form of ghee), nut-free, egg-free, or meatless, it will be indicated in the recipe's labels.

Recipe tips: Each recipe includes tips for ingredient substitution, recipe variations, or instructions on food prep and storage.

Macro percentages: All recipes include macro percentages as well as complete nutritional information.

Crustless Spinach Quiche, page 3

Chapter Two

EGGS AND BREAKFAST

Banana Noatmeal

DAIRY-FREE, EGG-FREE, MEATLESS

This low-carb recipe has no oats but is creamy, delicious, and very close to the real thing. It is topped with bananas and walnuts for added texture and flavor. I like to serve mine with extra almond milk on the cereal. It helps cool it down and thin the cereal some. This recipe will make you feel like you are eating the real thing, only this thing is better for you!

Serves 4   **Prep time: 5 minutes / Cook time: 3 minutes**

1 cup almond meal

3 tablespoons
  hemp seed

2 tablespoons ground
  flaxseed

2 tablespoons white
  chia seeds

2 cups almond milk,
  or coconut milk, plus
  more for serving
  (optional)

1 tablespoon
  banana extract

1 large banana, sliced
  and divided

4 tablespoons sugar-free
  maple syrup, divided

2 tablespoons chopped
  walnuts, divided

Ground cinnamon,
  for dusting

1. In a small saucepan over medium heat, stir together the almond meal, hemp seed, flaxseed, and chia seeds. Add the almond milk and banana extract and whisk until smooth. Simmer for 3 minutes.

2. Divide the cereal into serving bowls. Place one quarter of the banana in each bowl. Drizzle each bowl with 1 tablespoon of maple syrup and 1½ teaspoons of chopped walnuts.

3. Serve with ½ cup of almond milk (if desired) poured over the noatmeal and dust with cinnamon.

Substitution Tip: It's easy to modify this recipe to your liking. Substitute your favorite extract for the banana extract and top it with your favorite berries, nuts, nut butter, or seeds.

Per Serving

Macronutrients: 69% Fat, 14% Protein, 17% Carbs

Calories: 350; Total Fat: 27g; Saturated Fat: 2g; Protein: 12g; Total Carbs: 27g; Fiber: 22g; Net Carbs: 5g; Cholesterol: 0mg

Chocolate Chia Pudding Bowl

DAIRY-FREE, EGG-FREE, MEATLESS

The chia seeds make magic in your bowl when you combine them with coconut milk and a little sweetener. As they soak in liquid, they gel and thicken so the combination resembles a pudding. My children compare it to tapioca pudding in thickness and texture.

Serves 6   **Prep time: 5 minutes, plus overnight chilling**

2 cups coconut milk

¼ cup maple syrup

¼ cup sugar-free chocolate syrup

1 teaspoon almond extract

2 cups white chia seeds

Toasted coconut flakes, for serving (optional)

Sugar-free chocolate chips, for serving (optional)

1. In a large microwave-safe bowl, combine the coconut milk, maple syrup, chocolate syrup, and almond extract. Microwave on high power for 1 minute. Remove the bowl from the microwave and whisk until the chocolate syrup is completely dissolved in the coconut milk.

2. Stir in the chia seeds until well combined. Refrigerate for up to 24 hours.

3. Serve, topped with toasted coconut flakes (if using) and chocolate chips (if using).

   Ingredient Tip: Chia seeds can stick together. You can stir the seeds into the liquid well, and they will still settle. Because of this, I recommend stirring the seeds every now and then while they soak.

Per Serving

Macronutrients: 54% Fat, 14% Protein, 32% Carbs

Calories: 501; Total Fat: 30g; Saturated Fat: 12g; Protein: 17g; Total Carbs: 39g; Fiber: 27g; Net Carbs: 12g; Cholesterol: 0mg

Grain-Free Granola

DAIRY-FREE, EGG-FREE, MEATLESS

Hemp hearts are shelled hemp seeds and contain a whopping 10 grams of protein per serving. They have a nutty flavor and are rich in omega fatty acids, 3 and 6. I enjoy eating this granola on its own as a snack or as a topping on the Banana Noatmeal (page 22).

Serves 9   **Prep time: 10 minutes / Cook time: 45 minutes**

1 cup raw walnut halves

1 cup raw pecan halves

1 cup raw
   slivered almonds

½ cup hemp hearts

½ cup unsweetened
   coconut flakes

½ cup almond flour

1 teaspoon ground
   cinnamon

½ teaspoon fine sea salt

¼ cup maple syrup

3 tablespoons melted
   coconut oil

1 teaspoon vanilla extract

1. Preheat the oven to 300°F.

2. In a large bowl, stir together the walnuts, pecans, almonds, hemp hearts, coconut, almond flour, cinnamon, and salt. Mix well.

3. Add the maple syrup, melted coconut oil, and vanilla. Stir until the nut mixture is completely coated. Transfer the granola mixture to a large sheet pan.

4. Bake for 45 minutes, stirring every 15 minutes, or until the granola is golden brown.

5. Remove from the oven and let cool for 15 minutes. Stir the granola to break it up into bite-size chunks. Store in an airtight container in a cool dry area.

Substitution Tip: The only recommended substitution for the maple syrup is sugar-free maple syrup or honey. The stickiness of the syrup or honey is what helps make the granola clusters form.

Per Serving (½ cup)

Macronutrients: 82% Fat, 9% Protein, 9% Carbs

Calories: 297; Total Fat: 27g; Saturated Fat: 6g; Protein: 7g; Total Carbs: 11g; Fiber: 4g; Net Carbs: 7g; Cholesterol: 0mg

Lemon Blueberry Pancakes

DAIRY-FREE, MEATLESS

Blueberries are my favorite fruit and they are often labeled a superfood. They are high in fiber, vitamins C and K, and manganese. I make these lemon blueberry pancakes year-round. It is easy to substitute frozen blueberries for fresh. If doing so, add the blueberries to the batter while still frozen.

Serves 4   Prep time: 10 minutes / Cook time: 10 minutes

½ cup almond flour

¼ cup coconut flour

1 tablespoon ground flaxseed

1 teaspoon baking soda

½ teaspoon salt

3 large eggs

¼ cup almond milk

2 tablespoons freshly squeezed lemon juice

½ teaspoon grated lemon zest (optional)

1 tablespoon maple syrup

1 teaspoon vanilla extract

⅔ cup fresh blueberries

1. Preheat a large nonstick skillet over medium heat.

2. In a large bowl, whisk the almond flour, coconut flour, flaxseed, baking soda, and salt to combine.

3. Add the eggs, almond milk, lemon juice, lemon zest (if using), maple syrup, and vanilla to the flour mixture. Whisk until well combined. Gently fold the blueberries into the pancake batter.

4. Scoop ¼ cup of batter into the preheated skillet. Cook for 1 minute, or until the top begins to bubble and the edges begin to brown. Flip and cook for 1 minute more, or until cooked through. Serve as desired.

Ingredient Tip: Use a citrus zester or Microplane to zest the lemon. When zesting, move the lemon in one direction against the blade and only remove the yellow part. I always zest the lemon I am going to juice first, then extract the juice from that lemon. Freeze any unused lemon zest in a sealed container for future use.

Per Serving (2 pancakes)

Macronutrients: 52% Fat, 17% Protein, 31% Carbs

Calories: 206; Total Fat: 12g; Saturated Fat: 2g; Protein: 9g; Total Carbs: 16g; Fiber: 6g; Net Carbs: 10g; Cholesterol: 140mg

Apple Dutch Baby

DAIRY-FREE, MEATLESS

A Dutch baby is a large pancake baked in an ovenproof skillet. Thicker than a regular pancake, they're often enjoyed as a breakfast or brunch item, but can also be served as a dessert.

Serves 4   **Prep time: 15 minutes / Cook time: 30 minutes**

1 tablespoon coconut oil

3 cups thinly sliced Honeycrisp apple, divided

1 teaspoon ground cinnamon, divided

4 large eggs

¾ cup almond milk

1 tablespoon sugar-free maple syrup

2 teaspoons vanilla extract

¾ cup almond flour

2 tablespoons coconut flour

1½ tablespoons powdered erythritol, plus more for dusting (optional)

1. Preheat the oven to 425°F.

2. In a cast iron skillet over medium-high heat, melt the coconut oil. Add 2 cups of apple slices and sprinkle with ½ teaspoon of ground cinnamon. Simmer the apples for 2 minutes until they begin to soften.

3. While the apples simmer, in a large bowl, whisk the eggs, almond milk, maple syrup, and vanilla until combined.

4. Whisk in the almond flour and coconut flour until blended. Pour the pancake batter into the hot cast iron skillet covering the apples. Place the skillet in the hot oven.

5. Bake for 20 to 25 minutes until the pancake is puffy and no longer wet on top.

6. In a small bowl, stir together the powdered erythritol (if using) and the remaining ½ teaspoon of ground cinnamon and sprinkle the mixture over the Dutch baby.

7. Top with the remaining 1 cup of apple slices and dust with powdered erythritol (if using).

Substitution Tip: Reduce the carbs by substituting zucchini for the apples. Sauté 2 cups zucchini slices in a skillet with ½ teaspoon ground cinnamon and a spoonful of sugar-free maple syrup. Top with the remaining 1 cup of zucchini for serving.

Per Serving

Macronutrients: 61% Fat, 16% Protein, 23% Carbs

Calories: 293; Total Fat: 20; Saturated Fat: 5g; Protein: 12g; Total Carbs: 20g; Fiber: 6g; Net Carbs: 14g; Cholesterol: 186mg

Paleo Pumpkin Muffins

DAIRY-FREE, MEATLESS

Pumpkin is packed with vitamins and is particularly high in vitamin A and beta-carotene. It can help boost the immune system and fight infection. These muffins have a dense texture and are full of delicious pumpkin flavor. There are a lot of eggs in this recipe, but the coconut flour will absorb a lot of liquid, and the eggs are needed to help bind the ingredients.

Makes 12 muffins   **Prep time: 10 minutes / Cook time: 20 minutes**

½ cup almond flour
½ cup coconut flour
½ cup erythritol, or maple syrup
1 teaspoon ground cinnamon
½ teaspoon ground nutmeg
½ teaspoon salt
¼ teaspoon ground cloves
1 cup pumpkin purée
5 large eggs
1 teaspoon maple extract
2 tablespoons pumpkin seeds (optional)

1. Preheat the oven to 350°F. Line a 12-cup muffin pan with paper liners and set aside.

2. In a medium bowl, whisk the almond flour, coconut flour, erythritol, cinnamon, nutmeg, salt, and cloves to combine.

3. Add the pumpkin, eggs, and maple extract to the flour mixture. Stir to combine. Spoon the muffin batter into the prepared muffin cups, filling each cup three-quarters full.

4. Sprinkle a few pumpkin seeds (if using) on each muffin.

5. Bake for 20 minutes, or until a toothpick inserted into the center of a muffin comes out clean.

6. Remove from the oven and cool. Store in an airtight container.

Variation Tip: Stir in ½ cup sugar-free chocolate chips before portioning the batter into the muffin pan.

Per Serving (1 muffin)

Macronutrients: 54% Fat, 24% Protein, 22% Carbs

Calories: 84; Total Fat: 5g; Saturated Fat: 1g; Protein: 5g; Total Carbs: 6g; Fiber: 4g; Net Carbs: 2g; Cholesterol: 78mg

Raspberry Almond Breakfast Bars

DAIRY-FREE, EGG-FREE, MEATLESS

Eating Paleo means giving up convenience foods like prepackaged breakfast bars. Making a batch of these bars for the week will help you stay Paleo and make busy mornings easier. Almonds and cashews provide protein and the almond butter helps bind these no-cook bars together for a satisfyingly simple meal.

Makes 12 bars   **Prep time: 10 minutes, plus chilling time**

1 cup unsweetened shredded coconut

1 cup raw almonds

1 cup raw cashews

⅓ cup honey, plus 2 tablespoons (divided) (2 tablespoons optional)

¼ cup almond butter

¼ cup almond flour

¼ cup crushed freeze-dried raspberries

1. Line a loaf pan with parchment paper. Set aside.

2. In a food processor, combine the coconut, almonds, cashews, ⅓ cup of honey, almond butter, and almond flour. Pulse to combine. Add water, 1 tablespoon at a time, if needed, to bring the mixture together. Transfer the mixture to the prepared loaf pan and press it with a spatula until it is uniform on all sides. Refrigerate for 3 hours until firm.

3. Drizzle the mixture with the remaining 2 tablespoons of honey (if using) and sprinkle with the freeze-dried raspberries. Return to the refrigerator for 30 minutes more to allow the honey to stiffen. Cut into 12 bars and serve.

Substitution Tip: Substitute sugar-free maple syrup for the honey.

Per Serving
Macronutrients: 71% Fat, 10% Protein, 19% Carbs
Calories: 252; Total Fat: 20g; Saturated Fat: 6g; Protein: 6g; Total Carbs: 17g; Fiber: 4g; Net Carbs: 13g; Cholesterol: 0mg

Tomato Avocado Bacon Stacks with Creamy Ranch Dressing

DAIRY-FREE, EGG-FREE

Most creamy dressings are milk based, but this ranch-flavored dressing is completely dairy-free and full of flavor. Raw cashews are blended with water and herbs for a delicious dressing. Plus you can store it for up to a week and use on other salads.

Serves 4   Prep time: 15 minutes

For the creamy ranch dressing

1 cup raw cashew halves

1/2 cup water

1 tablespoon freshly squeezed lemon juice

1 teaspoon dried dill

1/2 teaspoon dried garlic powder

1/2 teaspoon dried onion powder

1/4 teaspoon freshly ground black pepper

1/2 teaspoon salt

For the tomato avocado bacon stacks

4 large tomatoes, each cut into 4 slices (16 slices total)

1 avocado, peeled, halved, pitted, and cut into 16 slices

4 cooked bacon slices, crumbled

1/4 cup chopped yellow bell pepper

To make the creamy ranch dressing

In a blender, combine the cashews, 1/2 cup water, lemon juice, dill, garlic powder, onion powder, pepper, and salt. Blend on high speed until smooth.

To make the tomato avocado bacon stacks

1. Arrange the tomato and avocado slices, alternating, on 4 serving plates.

2. Drizzle each plate with 2 tablespoons of dressing and evenly sprinkle with the bacon and yellow bell pepper.

Leftovers Tip: The creamy cashew dressing can be used on a salad or as a dip for your favorite veggies and chicken wings. Refrigerate any leftover dressing in an airtight jar for up to 1 week.

Per Serving (1 stack plus 2 tablespoons dressing)

Macronutrients: 65% Fat, 13% Protein, 22% Carbs

Calories: 358; Total Fat: 26g; Saturated Fat: 5g; Protein: 12g; Total Carbs: 25g; Fiber: 6g; Net Carbs: 19g; Cholesterol: 10mg

Southwest Eggs Scramble

MEATLESS

These scrambled eggs are packed with veggies and spices for a delicious breakfast plate. Add a side of your favorite fruit to complete the meal. I prefer to mix the eggs and seasoning in a bowl first. You can also whisk the eggs, milk, and spices in the skillet with the vegetables in step 3.

Serves 2   Prep time: 10 minutes / Cook time: 10 minutes

8 large eggs
½ cup almond milk
1½ teaspoons chili powder
½ teaspoon ground cumin
½ teaspoon garlic powder
Salt
Freshly ground black pepper
2 tablespoons ghee
½ cup halved cherry tomatoes
½ cup chopped red bell pepper
¼ cup chopped scallion, white and green parts
1 tablespoon chopped jalapeño pepper
1 avocado, peeled, halved, pitted, and sliced (optional)
Chopped fresh cilantro, for garnish (optional)

1. In a large bowl, whisk the eggs, almond milk, chili powder, cumin, and garlic powder to combine. Season with salt and pepper.

2. In a large nonstick skillet over medium heat, melt the ghee. Add the cherry tomatoes, red bell pepper, scallion, and jalapeño. Cook for 5 minutes, or until the vegetables are soft, stirring occasionally.

3. Add the whisked egg mixture and cook for 5 minutes, or until the eggs are cooked through, stirring and folding the eggs occasionally.

4. Taste and season with salt and pepper, as needed. Garnish with avocado slices (if using) and chopped cilantro (if using).

Ingredient Tip: Save time measuring spices by making a batch of the spice blend ahead. Combine 2 tablespoons chili powder, 2 teaspoons ground cumin, and 2 teaspoons garlic powder. Use 2½ teaspoons of the spice mix for this recipe.

Per Serving

Macronutrients: 60% Fat, 29% Protein, 11% Carbs

Calories: 373; Total Fat: 25g; Saturated Fat: 10g; Protein: 27g; Total Carbs: 9g; Fiber: 3g; Net Carbs: 6g; Cholesterol: 754mg

Egg and Asparagus Salad

MEATLESS, NUT-FREE

Asparagus stalks vary in thickness. If you use a thicker stalk, adjust the cooking time to 5 minutes, or until crisp-tender. To remove any tough woody ends, hold the asparagus stalk halfway down the spear and bend it until it snaps.

Serves 2   **Prep time: 10 minutes / Cook time: 10 minutes**

1 tablespoon freshly squeezed lemon juice

½ teaspoon grated lemon zest

¼ teaspoon salt

⅛ teaspoon freshly ground black pepper

3 teaspoons ghee, divided

2 tablespoons chopped shallot

1 bunch asparagus spears, trimmed

4 large eggs

1 teaspoon chopped fresh mint leaves (optional)

1. In a small bowl, whisk the lemon juice, lemon zest, salt, and pepper to combine. Set aside.

2. In a large nonstick skillet over medium, melt 1½ teaspoons of ghee.

3. Add the shallot and cook for 1 minute, or until translucent.

4. Place the asparagus in the skillet with the shallot and cook for 3 minutes, or until the asparagus is bright green and crisp-tender, tossing frequently.

5. Remove the asparagus from the skillet and divide it between serving plates.

6. Place the skillet over low heat and melt the remaining ghee. Crack the eggs into the skillet and fry for 3 to 5 minutes, until the egg whites have set and the yolks are thick but are not hard.

7. Place two eggs on top of the asparagus on each plate. Drizzle with the lemon juice mixture and garnish with fresh mint (if using).

Substitution Tip: Change the flavor profile: Swap the fresh mint for chopped fresh chives and sprinkle the finished product with cayenne pepper.

Per Serving
Macronutrients: 61% Fat, 27% Protein, 12% Carbs
Calories: 250; Total Fat: 17g; Saturated Fat: 7g; Protein: 17g; Total Carbs: 9g; Fiber: 4g; Net Carbs: 5g; Cholesterol: 389mg

Cauliflower Rice and Egg Bowl

MEATLESS, NUT-FREE

These visual and taste sensations are an egg lover's dream. The fried eggs' warm runny yolk drizzles into the cauliflower rice—don't forget a dash of sriracha, Creamy Ranch Dressing (page 30), or both.

Serves 4   Prep time: 10 minutes / Cook time: 20 minutes

2 tablespoons
  ghee, divided
4 cups cauliflower rice
1 teaspoon salt
½ teaspoon chili powder
2 cups fresh
  baby spinach
1 cup diced fire-roasted
  tomatoes
4 large eggs
1 avocado, peeled,
  halved, pitted,
  and sliced
1 tablespoon chopped
  fresh cilantro

1. In a large nonstick skillet over medium-high heat, melt 1 tablespoon of ghee.

2. Add the cauliflower rice, salt, and chili powder and toss to combine. Sauté the cauliflower for 10 minutes, or until it becomes browned and crispy.

3. Stir in the baby spinach and tomatoes. Cook for 2 minutes more, or until the spinach wilts and the tomatoes are warmed through.

4. Divide the cauliflower rice among serving bowls. Wipe the skillet clean with a paper towel.

5. Return the skillet to the heat and melt the remaining 1 tablespoon of ghee. Crack the eggs into the skillet and fry for 3 to 5 minutes, or until the egg whites are thick and the yolks have begun to thicken but are not hard.

6. Place 1 egg on each bowl of cauliflower rice and serve with the avocado and cilantro.

Ingredient Tip: Keeping the lid off the skillet allows air to circulate while cooking and stirring, resulting in tasty browned bits of cauliflower rice.

Per Serving

Macronutrients: 63% Fat, 21% Protein, 16% Carbs

Calories: 244; Total Fat: 17g; Saturated Fat: 6g; Protein: 13g; Total Carbs: 14g; Fiber: 7g; Net Carbs: 7g; Cholesterol: 201mg

Paleo Eggs Benedict

MEATLESS

Mushrooms replace the usual English muffin in this reworked Paleo version of a breakfast favorite. Mushrooms retain a lot of water, which releases during the cooking process. While the mushrooms sauté, the flavor intensifies as the water cooks down. For this reason, the mushrooms should be sautéed until the water is bubbly and starts to evaporate.

Serves 4   **Prep time: 10 minutes / Cook time: 10 minutes**

3 teaspoons
ghee, divided
4 large portobello
mushroom caps
4 large eggs
¼ cup Creamy Ranch
Dressing (page 30)
1 tablespoon chopped
fresh chives

1. In a large cast iron skillet over medium heat, heat 1½ teaspoons of ghee. Place the mushroom caps in the skillet and sauté for 2 minutes. Turn the mushrooms over and cook for 2 minutes more. Remove the mushrooms from the skillet and set aside on serving plates. Wipe the skillet clean with a paper towel.

2. Return the skillet to the heat and add the remaining 1½ teaspoons of ghee to melt.

3. Crack the eggs into the skillet and fry for 3 to 5 minutes until the whites have completely set. Flip the eggs over, if desired, and cook to your preferred level of doneness.

4. Place 1 egg on each mushroom cap. Drizzle with the dressing and sprinkle evenly with fresh chives.

   Option Tip: Stir some hot sauce into the ranch dressing before drizzling it over the eggs to give your eggs Benedict a spicy kick.

Per Serving
Macronutrients: 66% Fat, 32% Protein, 2% Carbs
Calories: 163; Total Fat: 12g; Saturated Fat: 4g; Protein: 13g; Total Carbs: 5g; Fiber: 1g; Net Carbs: 5g; Cholesterol: 192mg

Oven-Baked Western Omelet

Nutritional yeast flakes have a strong flavor that resembles cheese. I use it here to simulate the flavor of cheese used in a typical omelet. I promise you'll find this just as delicious. To get an even bigger flavor boost, drizzle with 1 tablespoon of Creamy Ranch Dressing (page 30) or salsa for an extra kick.

Serves 4   **Prep time: 10 minutes / Cook time: 50 minutes**

1 tablespoon ghee
1 cup chopped
 cooked ham
½ cup chopped green
 bell pepper
¼ cup chopped onion
8 large eggs
⅓ cup coconut milk
2 tablespoons nutritional
 yeast flakes (optional)
Chopped fresh chives,
 for garnish (optional)

1. Preheat the oven to 350°F.

2. In a large nonstick skillet over medium heat, melt the ghee. Add the ham, green bell pepper, and onion. Sauté for 5 minutes, or until the onion begins to look translucent.

3. In a large bowl, whisk the eggs, coconut milk, and nutritional yeast flakes (if using). Pour the egg mixture into the skillet and transfer the skillet to the oven.

4. Bake for 45 minutes, or until the eggs are cooked and the omelet is set. Serve garnished with fresh chives (if using).

Substitution Tip: Substitute 6 bacon slices for the ham. Cook the bacon, then remove from the skillet along with all but 1 tablespoon of bacon grease. Proceed to step 2 and sauté the bell pepper and onion. The bacon is crumbled and stirred into the egg mixture in step 3, then finish as instructed.

Per Serving

Macronutrients: 64% Fat, 27% Protein, 9% Carbs

Calories: 281; Total Fat: 20g; Saturated Fat: 10g; Protein: 19g; Total Carbs: 4g; Fiber: <1g; Net Carbs: 3g; Cholesterol: 399mg

Crustless Spinach Quiche

DAIRY-FREE, MEATLESS

This spinach quiche makes a great addition to a weekend morning brunch with a side of your favorite fruit salad. Leftovers reheat well and are a good option for a portable lunch. I also like to make this recipe with broccoli. Just substitute 2 cups chopped steamed broccoli florets for the spinach.

Serves 4   **Prep time: 10 minutes / Cook time: 30 minutes**

Coconut oil, for
   preparing the
   baking dish
6 large eggs
½ cup coconut milk
¼ cup chopped onion
¼ cup coconut flour
2 garlic cloves, minced
½ teaspoon
   baking powder
½ teaspoon salt
¼ teaspoon freshly
   ground black pepper
2 cups chopped
   fresh spinach

1. Preheat the oven to 350°F. Lightly coat a round casserole dish with coconut oil.

2. In a large bowl, whisk the eggs, coconut milk, onion, coconut flour, garlic, baking powder, salt, and pepper until well combined.

3. Stir in the spinach. Transfer the egg mixture to the prepared casserole dish.

4. Bake for 30 minutes, or until the edges have browned and the egg is cooked through.

Cooking Tip: This recipe calls for a round casserole dish. A 9-inch glass pie dish can be used, if needed. To gauge doneness, look at the top of the quiche. If it still looks wet and is jiggly, it is not ready. When the quiche is no longer wet on top, slide a knife into the center of the quiche. If it comes out clean, it is cooked through.

Per Serving

Macronutrients: 64% Fat, 27% Protein, 9% Carbs

Calories: 210; Total Fat: 15g; Saturated Fat: 9g; Protein: 14g; Total Carbs: 9g; Fiber: 4g; Net Carbs: 5g; Cholesterol: 278mg

Butternut Squash and Sausage Frittata

DAIRY-FREE, NUT-FREE

This is one of my favorite frittata recipes. I usually make it for special occasions, but it's just too delicious to enjoy only once in a while. The spicy sausage and sweet butternut squash combine into a delicious blend of flavors. If spicy sausage isn't your thing, use sweet Italian sausage instead.

Serves 4   **Prep time: 15 minutes / Cook time: 40 minutes**

8 ounces hot Italian sausage

1 cup chopped peeled butternut squash

½ cup chopped onion

½ cup chopped red bell pepper

6 large eggs

1 teaspoon Italian seasoning

½ teaspoon garlic powder

½ teaspoon salt

½ teaspoon freshly ground black pepper

1. Heat a large cast iron skillet over medium heat until hot.

2. Crumble the sausage into the skillet and cook for 10 minutes, or until the sausage is cooked through and no longer pink. Remove the sausage from the skillet and set aside, leaving the grease in the skillet.

3. Return the skillet to the heat and add the butternut squash, onion, and red bell pepper. Cook for 15 minutes, stirring occasionally, or until the butternut squash is easily pierced with a fork. Keep warm over low heat.

4. Preheat the broiler.

5. In a large bowl, whisk the eggs, Italian seasoning, garlic powder, salt, and pepper until well combined.

6. Return the sausage to the skillet and stir to combine with the butternut squash mixture. Turn the heat to medium.

7. Pour the eggs over the sausage mixture and cook for 5 minutes, or until the edges start to brown. Transfer the skillet to the oven.

8. Broil for 5 minutes until the frittata is puffed and brown on top.

Substitution Tip: Sweet potato can be used in place of butternut squash in this recipe. This also works well with summer squash, such as zucchini and yellow crookneck squash. You will need 2 cups of summer squash for the frittata and, in step 3, the squash will cook for 10 minutes, or until it just begins to soften.

Per Serving

Macronutrients: 62% Fat, 29% Protein, 9% Carbs

Calories: 317; Total Fat: 22g; Saturated Fat: 8g; Protein: 23g; Total Carbs: 10g; Fiber: 2g; Net Carbs: 8g; Cholesterol: 319mg

Sweet Potato Hash and Eggs

DAIRY-FREE, NUT-FREE

I found that shredding the sweet potatoes for this recipe helps it cook faster and creates crispy bits in the hash. You may opt to dice the potatoes, but this will add to your cook time.

Serves 4   **Prep time: 15 minutes / Cook time: 30 minutes**

8 thick-cut bacon slices
2 large sweet potatoes, peeled and shredded
¼ cup sliced scallion, white part only
2 garlic cloves, minced
2 cups roughly chopped fresh spinach
4 large eggs
Salt
Freshly ground black pepper
1 teaspoon smoked paprika
1 avocado, peeled, halved, pitted, and sliced (optional)
2 tablespoons chopped fresh cilantro (optional)

1. In a large nonstick skillet over medium heat, cook the bacon for 10 minutes until crispy. Remove the bacon from the skillet and set aside. Remove all but 1 tablespoon of bacon grease from the skillet.

2. Place the skillet over medium-high heat and add the sweet potatoes, scallion, and garlic. Stir to combine. Sauté for 6 minutes, or until the sweet potatoes begin to brown. Stir the potato mixture and sauté for 6 minutes more, or until the sweet potatoes are cooked through and have crispy edges.

3. Turn the heat to medium-low. Break an egg over each quarter section of the sweet potato hash.

4. Season with salt, pepper, and paprika. Cover the skillet and cook for 3 to 5 minutes until the egg whites have completely set and the yolks have begun to thicken but are not hard.

5. Serve with bacon and avocado on the side. Garnish with cilantro (if using).

Ingredient Tip: I like to bake extra sweet potatoes when making them for a meal, then refrigerate until ready to use. If using a precooked sweet potato, it should be diced instead of shredded.

Per Serving
Macronutrients: 48% Fat, 23% Protein, 29% Carbs
Calories: 302; Total Fat: 16g; Saturated Fat: 6g; Protein: 17g; Total Carbs: 21g; Fiber: 4g; Net Carbs: 17g; Cholesterol: 211mg

Brazilian Fish Stew, page 61

Chapter Three

SOUPS AND STEWS

Chicken Zoodle Soup

EGG-FREE, NUT-FREE

Veggie noodles are the noodle of choice on grain-free diets and have become a mainstay of the Paleo diet as "the" pasta noodle substitute. The zucchini noodles (a.k.a. zoodles) used in this recipe do not need to be cooked. Raw zucchini noodles will remain firm and have a toothsome bite similar to pasta. Because they can be very long and difficult to serve, chop them into smaller pieces before adding to the soup.

Serves 6   **Prep time: 15 minutes / Cook time: 25 minutes**

2 tablespoons ghee
2 pounds chicken thighs, cut into bite-size pieces
2 cups chopped mushrooms
½ cup thinly sliced carrot
2 garlic cloves, minced
1 teaspoon dried thyme
1 teaspoon salt
½ teaspoon freshly ground black pepper
6 cups chicken broth
3 cups zucchini noodles

1. In a large stockpot over medium-high heat, melt the ghee.

2. Add the chicken, mushrooms, carrot, garlic, thyme, salt, and pepper. Sauté for 5 minutes, stirring occasionally, or until the mushrooms have released their water and the chicken is no longer pink.

3. Add the chicken broth to the pot and bring it to a boil. Reduce the heat and simmer the soup for 15 minutes.

4. Add the zucchini noodles to the soup and serve immediately.

Ingredient Tip: This recipe can also be made using ground beef in place of the chicken. Just replace the 2 pounds of chicken with 1½ pounds of ground beef.

Per Serving

Macronutrients: 39% Fat, 53% Protein, 8% Carbs

Calories: 370; Total Fat: 16g; Saturated Fat: 6g; Protein: 49g; Total Carbs: 4g; Fiber: 1g; Net Carbs: 3g; Cholesterol: 207mg

Shrimp Pho Soup

EGG-FREE, NUT-FREE

It's easy to stay Paleo when you skip the takeout and pasta by making this flavorful pho for dinner right at home. I always loved takeout pho and I especially loved the noodles. In this recipe, I use shirataki noodles to substitute. Although they aren't as long as a pho noodle, they are still delicious and work great in this recipe. If one of the reasons you loved pho was the noodles, then the shirataki noodles come to the rescue here, making this version taste close to a takeout recipe.

Serves 4   Prep time: 15 minutes / Cook time: 10 minutes

1 tablespoon ghee

1 pound raw shrimp, peeled and deveined

1 teaspoon salt

½ teaspoon freshly ground black pepper

½ teaspoon red pepper flakes

½ teaspoon garlic powder

6 cups chicken broth

1 teaspoon grated peeled fresh ginger

1 (6-ounce) package shirataki noodles, drained and rinsed

Fresh basil leaves, for garnish (optional)

Jalapeño pepper slices, for garnish (optional)

Lime wedges, for serving (optional)

1. In a large stockpot over medium-high heat, melt the ghee. Add the shrimp, salt, pepper, red pepper flakes, and garlic powder. Cook the shrimp for 5 minutes, stirring occasionally, or until the shrimp just turn opaque.

2. Add the chicken broth and ginger. Bring the soup to a boil, then remove from the heat.

3. Stir in the shirataki noodles.

4. Serve topped with basil (if using) and jalapeño (if using), with lime wedges (if using) on the side for squeezing.

Ingredient Tip: Save even more time by buying precooked shrimp. Just thaw the shrimp and add it to the soup in step 2.

Per Serving

Macronutrients: 33% Fat, 58% Protein, 9% Carbs

Calories: 137; Total Fat: 5g; Saturated Fat: 2g; Protein: 20g; Total Carbs: 4g; Fiber: 1g; Net Carbs: 3g; Cholesterol: 153mg

Paleo Egg Drop Soup

DAIRY-FREE

This Paleo egg drop soup is super-fast to prepare and ready in just 10 minutes. It is low enough in carbs and calories that you could enjoy two servings without going overboard. It is made with bone broth, which is similar to stock, only it is simmered longer to extract the gelatin from the bones as well as release their collagen and nutrients.

Serves 4   **Prep time: 10 minutes / Cook time: 10 minutes**

6 cups chicken
   bone broth
1 tablespoon
   coconut aminos
1 teaspoon grated peeled
   fresh ginger
4 large eggs
4 scallions, thinly sliced,
   white and green parts

1. In a large stockpot over medium heat, combine the bone broth, coconut aminos, and ginger. Bring to a boil.

2. In a small bowl, whisk the eggs to combine.

3. Remove the broth from the heat and gently stir it while pouring the egg into the hot broth. Transfer the soup to serving bowls and garnish with scallions.

Ingredient Tip: If needed, chicken broth can be substituted for the bone broth with similar results.

Per Serving

Macronutrients: 36% Fat, 54% Protein, 10% Carbs

Calories: 148; Total Fat: 6g; Saturated Fat: 2g; Protein: 20g; Total Carbs: 2g; Fiber: 0g; Net Carbs: 2g; Cholesterol: 186mg

Ham and Green Bean Soup

EGG-FREE, NUT-FREE

Ham and green bean soup usually includes potatoes—a restricted ingredient in a Paleo diet. You can easily substitute radishes for potatoes in this recipe. They will take on a mild flavor and cook very much like a potato. Depending on the size of the radish, halve or quarter them for this recipe.

Serves 4   Prep time: 15 minutes / Cook time: 15 minutes

1 tablespoon ghee
½ cup chopped onion
2 garlic cloves, minced
1 (8-ounce) package radishes, halved or quartered
6 cups chicken broth
4 cups green beans, cut into 1-inch pieces
2 cups chopped cooked ham
Salt
Freshly ground black pepper

1. In a large stockpot over medium heat, melt the ghee. Add the onion and garlic and cook for 5 minutes, or until the onion is softened.

2. Add the radishes and cook for 5 minutes more, stirring occasionally.

3. Stir in the chicken broth, green beans, and ham. Bring the soup to a boil. Reduce the heat to maintain a simmer and cook for 5 minutes, or until the beans are fork-tender.

4. Taste and season with salt and pepper.

Ingredient Tip: The ham can also be bought diced and frozen beans can be substituted for fresh green beans, reducing prep time.

Per Serving

Macronutrients: 38% Fat, 51% Protein, 11% Carbs

Calories: 237; Total Fat: 10g; Saturated Fat: 3g; Protein: 30g; Total Carbs: 8g; Fiber: 2g; Net Carbs: 6g; Cholesterol: 73mg

Vegetable Broth Bowl

DAIRY-FREE, EGG-FREE, MEATLESS

The turmeric in this recipe is what adds color to the broth. The curcumin in turmeric is known to help fight inflammation, Chrohn's disease, irritable bowel syndrome, and ulcers. This vegetable broth bowl is not only good for you but also full of color and flavor. It is delicious on its own or as an accompaniment to chicken or seafood.

Serves 4 Prep time: 15 minutes / Cook time: 10 minutes

6 cups vegetable broth
½ teaspoon ground
  turmeric
½ teaspoon
  garlic powder
½ teaspoon
  onion powder
2 cups chopped kale
1 cup sliced mushrooms
1 cup assorted
  zucchini noodles
½ cup butternut
  squash noodles
½ cup carrot noodles
Coconut aminos, for
  serving (optional)

1. In a large stockpot over medium heat, stir together the vegetable broth, turmeric, garlic powder, and onion powder to combine. Cook for about 10 minutes until the broth comes to a boil. Remove from the heat.

2. Divide the kale, mushrooms, and zucchini, squash, and carrot noodles between 4 large soup bowls.

3. Pour 1½ cups of broth over the vegetables in each bowl. Let sit for 2 minutes to allow the ingredients to warm and soften. Serve with coconut aminos (if using).

Ingredient Tip: The assorted veggie noodles can be anything you wish—sweet potato, butternut squash, zucchini, or carrot, to name a few. Many varieties of already-prepared veggie noodles can now be found in the refrigerated produce section of most grocery stores.

Per Serving

Macronutrients: 14% Fat, 19% Protein, 67% Carbs

Calories: 64; Total Fat: 1g; Saturated Fat: 0g; Protein: 3g; Total Carbs: 13g; Fiber: 4g; Net Carbs: 9g; Cholesterol: 0mg

Tomato Cauliflower Rice Soup

DAIRY-FREE, EGG-FREE, MEATLESS, NUT-FREE

Whenever my husband is feeling under the weather, he likes to have this soup. It is my take on canned tomato rice soup, which was a comfort food for him before going low carb. Frozen cauliflower rice can be used in place of fresh, adjusting the sauté time in step 3 to 3 minutes.

Serves 4 **Prep time: 10 minutes / Cook time: 30 minutes**

1 tablespoon extra-virgin olive oil

1 carrot, chopped

¼ cup chopped onion

2 garlic cloves, minced

2 cups cauliflower rice

2 (14.5-ounce) cans diced tomatoes

3 cups vegetable broth

1½ teaspoons freshly squeezed lemon juice

1 teaspoon erythritol or honey (optional)

1 teaspoon Italian seasoning

1 teaspoon salt

¼ teaspoon freshly ground black pepper

1 tablespoon chopped fresh basil (optional)

1. In a large stockpot over medium heat, heat the olive oil until hot.

2. Add the carrot, onion, and garlic. Sauté for 5 minutes, or until lightly browned.

3. Stir in the cauliflower. Sauté for 5 minutes more, stirring occasionally.

4. Stir in the tomatoes and their juices, vegetable broth, lemon juice, erythritol (if using), Italian seasoning, salt, and pepper. Bring the soup to a boil. Reduce the heat to maintain a simmer and cook for 20 minutes until the vegetables soften and the flavors have combined.

5. Garnish with fresh basil (if using) and serve.

Substitution Tip: The sweetener is added to this soup to help cut the acid from the tomatoes. As the sweetener is optional, it is not included in the nutritional information. If using erythritol, the nutrition information remains unchanged. Honey increases the calories to 114, carbs to 16, and net carbs to 12.

Per Serving

Macronutrients: 33% Fat, 11% Protein, 56% Carbs

Calories: 109; Total Fat: 4g; Saturated Fat: 1g; Protein: 3g; Total Carbs: 14g; Fiber: 4g; Net Carbs: 10g; Cholesterol: 0mg

Pizza Soup

DAIRY-FREE, EGG-FREE, NUT-FREE

Pizza is a no-no in the Paleo world. I created this recipe to provide all the flavors of our favorite pie, but without the gluten. If you feel the need for a side dish, a simple salad with a Paleo-friendly salad dressing is the perfect touch. Feel free to use ground pork, chicken, turkey, or venison in this recipe in place of the beef and sausage.

Serves 6   Prep time: 15 minutes / Cook time: 25 minutes

8 ounces ground beef, crumbled

8 ounces ground sausage, crumbled

2 ounces sliced uncured pepperoni

4 cups beef broth

4 cups sliced mushrooms

1 (14.5-ounce) can crushed tomatoes

1 (15-ounce) can tomato sauce

¼ cup chopped onion

2 garlic cloves, minced

1 tablespoon Italian seasoning

1 teaspoon salt

½ teaspoon red pepper flakes (optional)

Fresh basil, for garnish (optional)

1. Select Sauté on the Instant Pot. Once hot, cook the beef, sausage, and pepperoni for 5 minutes, or until the beef and sausage have browned. Drain the excess fat, if desired.

2. Add the beef broth, mushrooms, crushed tomatoes, tomato sauce, onion, garlic, Italian seasoning, salt, and red pepper flakes (if using).

3. Lock the lid into place and seal the vent. Select Manual and cook on High Pressure for 20 minutes.

4. After cooking, quick release the pressure. Carefully unlock and remove the lid.

5. Garnish with fresh basil (if using) and serve.

Slow Cooker Tip: It is easy to convert this to a slow cooker recipe. Just add all the ingredients to the slow cooker, stir to mix well, cover the cooker, and cook on high heat for 3 to 4 hours, or low heat for 6 to 8 hours.

Per Serving

Macronutrients: 57% Fat, 30% Protein, 13% Carbs

Calories: 332; Total Fat: 21g; Saturated Fat: 8g; Protein: 25g; Total Carbs: 11g; Fiber: 3g; Net Carbs: 8g; Cholesterol: 62mg

Creamy Chicken Mushroom Soup

DAIRY-FREE, EGG-FREE

Mushrooms are high in antioxidants and rich in vitamins B and D as well as selenium. These nutrients support the immune system and can prevent damage to cells and tissues as well as aid in heart health. Mushrooms are an excellent food source for fiber.

Serves 4   **Prep time: 10 minutes / Cook time: 35 minutes**

1 tablespoon extra-virgin olive oil

8 ounces boneless, skinless chicken thighs

1/2 teaspoon salt

1/2 teaspoon freshly ground black pepper

12 ounces chopped mushrooms

1/4 cup chopped onion

1 teaspoon minced garlic

1/2 teaspoon dried thyme

1/2 teaspoon dried rosemary

4 cups chicken broth

1/3 cup coconut cream

1. In a large stockpot over medium heat, heat the olive oil. Season the chicken thighs on both sides with salt and pepper and add them to the hot oil. Cook for 6 minutes per side, or until the chicken is no longer pink. Remove the chicken from the pot and set aside.

2. Add the mushrooms, onion, garlic, thyme, and rosemary to the pot. Sauté for 5 minutes, until the mushrooms soften.

3. While the vegetables cook, cut the chicken thighs into bite-size pieces and place them back in the pot.

4. Add the chicken broth and bring it to a boil. Reduce the heat to maintain a simmer and cook for 15 minutes.

5. Stir in the coconut cream and heat for 2 minutes more before serving.

Ingredient Tip: Be sure to shake the can of coconut cream to mix it with the coconut water in the can before measuring for optimal results.

Per Serving

Macronutrients: 38% Fat, 38% Protein, 24% Carbs

Calories: 168; Total Fat: 7g; Saturated Fat: 2g; Protein: 16g; Total Carbs: 11g; Fiber: 1g; Net Carbs: 10g; Cholesterol: 47mg

Chicken Taco Soup

DAIRY-FREE, EGG-FREE

I think one of the biggest misconceptions about the Paleo diet is that you won't be able to eat rich and creamy foods. But dairy-free doesn't mean you'll miss richly flavored soups. The coconut cream in this recipe complements the spice and has a real comfort food feel. This is a great meal to prepare ahead, as it reheats easily. Be sure the salsa is Paleo approved.

Serves 4   Prep time: 15 minutes / Cook time: 20 minutes

1 pound chicken
   breast tenders
3 cups chicken broth
1 cup salsa
1½ teaspoons
   chili powder
1 teaspoon ground cumin
½ teaspoon paprika
½ teaspoon
   onion powder
½ teaspoon
   garlic powder
½ teaspoon salt
¼ teaspoon freshly
   ground black pepper
1 (14-ounce) can
   coconut cream
¼ cup chopped fresh
   cilantro (optional)
1 avocado, peeled,
   halved, pitted, and
   sliced (optional)
1 jalapeño pepper,
   sliced (optional)
1 lime, cut into wedges
   (optional)

1. In the Instant Pot, combine the chicken, chicken broth, salsa, chili powder, cumin, paprika, onion powder, garlic powder, salt, and pepper.

2. Lock the lid into place and seal the vent. Select Manual and cook on High Pressure for 15 minutes.

3. After cooking, let the pressure release naturally for 10 minutes, then quick release any remaining pressure. Carefully unlock and remove the lid. Remove the chicken and shred it with a fork. Set aside.

4. On the Instant Pot, select Sauté. Whisk in the coconut cream.

5. Return the shredded chicken to the pot. Bring the mixture to a boil and simmer for 3 to 4 minutes until the broth has reduced slightly.

6. Serve, topped with the optional ingredients as desired, and with lime wedges (if using) for squeezing.

Substitution Tip: Coconut milk can be used in place of coconut cream. The soup should simmer on Sauté a little longer, to reduce the broth, as the coconut milk is thinner than the cream. Alternatively, whisk in 1 tablespoon coconut flour, then simmer as directed. This will help thicken the soup.

Slow Cooker Tip: This can easily be converted to a slow cooker recipe: Place all the ingredients from step 1 in the crock, cover the cooker, and cook on high heat for 4 hours. Then, proceed with step 4, turn the slow cooker to high again, and continue as instructed.

Per Serving

Macronutrients: 56% Fat, 35% Protein, 9% Carbs

Calories: 323; Total Fat: 20g; Saturated Fat: 16g; Protein: 28g; Total Carbs: 6g; Fiber: 2g; Net Carbs: 4g; Cholesterol: 69mg

Butternut Squash and Bacon Soup

DAIRY-FREE, EGG-FREE, NUT-FREE

Naturally sweet butternut squash pairs well with smoky, salty bacon for a delicious sweet and savory soup. This soup is higher in carbs than most recipes in this cookbook and so should be enjoyed as an occasional treat.

Serves 6   **Prep time: 15 minutes / Cook time: 30 minutes**

6 thick-cut bacon slices, halved crosswise

6 large sage leaves, finely chopped

6 cups chopped peeled butternut squash

4 cups chicken broth

1 teaspoon salt

½ teaspoon freshly ground black pepper

1. In a large stockpot over medium heat, cook the bacon for 8 minutes, or until crispy. Remove from the stockpot and set aside on a paper towel to drain.

2. Increase the heat to medium-high. Add the sage and cook, stirring, for 1 minute. Add the butternut squash to the pot and cook for 6 minutes, or until lightly browned.

3. Stir in the chicken broth, salt, and pepper. Increase the heat to high and bring the soup to a boil. Reduce the heat to maintain a simmer and cook for 10 minutes, or until the squash is soft.

4. Using a potato masher, mash the squash into the soup. Serve with bacon crumbled over the top.

Substitution Tip: Save time and substitute 2 (12-ounce) packages frozen cooked squash purée for the fresh butternut squash in step 2. Continue to cook as instructed and skip step 4.

Per Serving

Macronutrients: 26% Fat, 23% Protein, 51% Carbs

Calories: 171; Total Fat: 5g; Saturated Fat: 2g; Protein: 10g; Total Carbs: 26g; Fiber: 8g; Net Carbs: 18g; Cholesterol: 12mg

Curried Shrimp and Sweet Potato Soup

EGG-FREE, NUT-FREE

Curry powder is a combination of turmeric, chili powder, coriander, cumin, ginger, and pepper. It can be mild, medium, or hot. This soup is warm and comforting on a chilly day. The curry-crusted shrimp are loaded with flavor and the optional jalapeño garnish adds an extra special touch of warmth—if you want to turn up the heat.

Serves 6   Prep time: 15 minutes / Cook time: 50 minutes

2 tablespoons
  ghee, divided
8 ounces raw shrimp,
  peeled and deveined
3 tablespoons yellow
  curry powder, divided
1 cup chopped
  sweet potato
½ cup chopped onion
½ cup chopped carrot
3 garlic cloves, minced
4 cups chicken broth
½ teaspoon salt
1 (13.5-ounce) can
  coconut milk
2 tablespoons chopped
  fresh cilantro (optional)
Jalapeño pepper slices,
  for garnish (optional)

1. In a large stockpot over medium heat, melt 1 tablespoon of ghee until hot. Add the shrimp and 1 tablespoon of curry powder. Cook for 7 minutes until the shrimp become opaque and have a cooked-on curry powder crust. Remove the shrimp from the stockpot.

2. Add the remaining 1 tablespoon of ghee to the pot to melt.

3. Add the sweet potato, onion, carrot, garlic, and remaining 2 tablespoons of curry powder. Cook for 10 minutes, stirring occasionally, or until the sweet potato softens.

4. Add the chicken broth and salt and bring to a boil. Reduce the heat to maintain a simmer and cook, uncovered, for 30 minutes, or until the vegetables are tender.

CONTINUED

Curried Shrimp and Sweet Potato Soup, CONTINUED

5. Stir in the coconut milk.

6. Ladle the soup into serving bowls and divide the shrimp evenly between them, placing the shrimp on top of the soup. Garnish with cilantro (if using), and jalapeño slices (if using).

Ingredient Tip: Purchase precooked shrimp to save cooking time. After the shrimp are thawed, toss them into the ghee and curry powder and cook for 2 minutes to warm the shrimp and coat them with the curry and ghee.

Per Serving

Macronutrients: 63% Fat, 16% Protein, 21% Carbs

Calories: 256; Total Fat: 18g; Saturated Fat: 14g; Protein: 10g; Total Carbs: 13g; Fiber: 2g; Net Carbs: 11g; Cholesterol: 58mg

Curried Cauliflower Chowder

DAIRY-FREE, EGG-FREE, NUT-FREE

This simple chowder uses the convenience of frozen cauliflower to save on prep and cooking time. If you prefer to use fresh cauliflower, substitute 2 cups cauliflower florets and increase the cook time to 10 minutes, or until the cauliflower is fork-tender.

Serves 4   **Prep time: 10 minutes / Cook time: 25 minutes**

2 tablespoons
extra-virgin olive oil

½ cup chopped onion

1 (12-ounce) bag frozen
cauliflower florets

1 teaspoon yellow
curry powder

½ teaspoon
ground cumin

½ teaspoon ground
turmeric

3 cups chicken broth

1 cup coconut milk

Salt

Freshly ground
black pepper

Chopped fresh parsley,
for garnish (optional)

1. In a large stockpot over medium heat, heat the olive oil until hot. Add the onion and sauté for 3 minutes, or until translucent.

2. Add the cauliflower and cook for 5 minutes until the cauliflower has thawed. Stir in the curry powder, cumin, and turmeric.

3. Stir in the chicken broth and bring the soup to a boil. Reduce the heat to maintain a simmer and cook for 10 minutes, or until the cauliflower is fork-tender.

4. Using a potato masher, mash the cauliflower in the pot to break it up into smaller pieces.

5. Stir in the coconut milk. Bring the soup back to the boiling point and remove it from the heat. Taste and season with salt and pepper. Garnish with parsley (if using) to serve.

Option Tip: Add some protein to your bowl by using 1 cup chopped cooked ham in the soup, or crumbled bacon pieces to garnish.

Per Serving
Macronutrients: 79% Fat, 8% Protein, 13% Carbs
Calories: 204; Total Fat: 18g; Saturated Fat: 11g; Protein: 4g; Total Carbs: 9g; Fiber: 1g; Net Carbs: 8g; Cholesterol: 4mg

Vegetable Chowder

DAIRY-FREE, EGG-FREE, MEATLESS

A chowder typically includes potatoes. However, in a Paleo diet, cauliflower, and radishes are common ingredients used to replace potatoes in recipes such as this chowder. The vegetables have texture and creaminess but are much lower in carbs. Plus, you'll get the added boost of vitamins C and K, potassium, and calcium.

Serves 6   **Prep time: 15 minutes / Cook time: 1 hour**

1 tablespoon coconut oil
4 carrots, chopped
½ yellow onion, chopped
2 garlic cloves, minced
4 cups chopped
   cauliflower
2 cups sliced mushrooms
4 celery stalks, chopped
1 cup sliced radishes
4 cups vegetable broth
1 teaspoon Italian
   seasoning
1 teaspoon salt
½ teaspoon freshly
   ground black pepper
¼ cup coconut cream

1. In a large stockpot over medium heat, melt the coconut oil. Add the carrots, onion, and garlic. Sauté for 3 minutes, or until fragrant.

2. Add the cauliflower, mushrooms, celery, and radishes. Sauté for 15 minutes, stirring frequently, until the vegetables are tender.

3. Pour in the vegetable broth and add the Italian seasoning, salt, and pepper. Bring the soup to a boil, then reduce the heat to maintain a simmer. Cook the soup for 30 minutes.

4. Stir in the coconut cream and simmer for 5 minutes more before serving.

Substitution Tip: Swap out 2 cups of the cauliflower for 2 cups of broccoli to add another layer of flavor and color to this chowder.

Per Serving
Macronutrients: 48% Fat, 14% Protein, 38% Carbs
Calories: 112; Total Fat: 6g; Saturated Fat: 5g; Protein: 4g; Total Carbs: 13g; Fiber: 4g; Net Carbs: 9g; Cholesterol: 0mg

Seafood Chowder

DAIRY-FREE, EGG-FREE

We are big fans of seafood in my house, and my hubby's favorite soup to order when eating out has always been clam chowder, so I decided to come up with a way to make him happy without the potatoes. This recipe is not as thick as a traditional chowder. If you feel the need for a thicker chowder, in step 4, dissolve 2 teaspoons arrowroot powder in the coconut milk and simmer for 3 minutes until it has thickened.

Serves 6   **Prep time: 10 minutes / Cook time: 20 minutes**

2 tablespoons
  coconut oil

2 cups radishes,
  quartered

½ small onion, chopped

3 garlic cloves, minced

8 ounces small raw
  shrimp, peeled and
  deveined

1 pound cod,
  roughly chopped

2 cups chicken broth

1 teaspoon salt

½ teaspoon freshly
  ground black pepper

1½ cups coconut milk

1. In a large stockpot over medium heat, heat the coconut oil. Add the radishes, onion, and garlic. Sauté for 3 minutes, or until the onion is soft.

2. Add the shrimp to the pot and cook, stirring often, for 5 minutes.

3. Add the cod, chicken broth, salt, and pepper to the pot. Cover the pot and bring the soup to a boil. Reduce the heat to maintain a simmer and cook for 7 minutes, or until the cod flakes easily with a fork.

4. Stir in the coconut milk and bring the broth back to a boil. Remove from the heat and serve.

Ingredient Tip: Purchase already peeled and deveined shrimp to save prep time.

Per Serving

Macronutrients: 54% Fat, 36% Protein, 10% Carbs

Calories: 266; Total Fat: 16g; Saturated Fat: 13g; Protein: 24g; Total Carbs: 5g; Fiber: 1g; Net Carbs: 4g; Cholesterol: 92mg

Thai Chicken Stew

DAIRY-FREE, EGG-FREE

This recipe calls for fish sauce, which is a staple in Thai-style cooking. It's shelf-stable at room temperature for up to four years. Coconut aminos are a good substitute. The flavor profile will change a bit because coconut aminos are slightly sweet.

Serves 6   **Prep time: 15 minutes / Cook time: 4 hours**

1 (13.5-ounce) can coconut milk

1 tablespoon grated peeled fresh ginger

1 tablespoon green curry paste

1 teaspoon fish sauce

½ teaspoon salt

¼ teaspoon freshly ground black pepper

3 pounds boneless, skinless chicken thighs, chopped

1 cup sliced radishes

½ onion, chopped

2 tablespoons chopped fresh cilantro (optional)

4 lime wedges (optional)

1. In a slow cooker, whisk the coconut milk, ginger, curry paste, fish sauce, salt, and pepper. Add the chicken thighs, radishes, and onion.

2. Cover the cooker and cook on low heat for 4 hours.

3. Garnish with fresh cilantro (if using) and serve with lime wedges (if using) for squeezing.

Option Tip: If desired, serve this stew over steamed cauliflower rice or raw zucchini noodles.

Instant Pot Tip: Place the chicken thighs in the bottom of the inner pot. Pour the coconut milk over the chicken. Add the ginger, curry paste, fish sauce, salt, and pepper. Lock the lid in place and seal the vent. Select Manual and cook on High Pressure for 15 minutes. Quick release the pressure, then carefully unlock and remove the lid. Stir in the radishes and onion. Lock the lid in place and seal the vent. Select Manual and cook on Low for 2 minutes. Quick release the pressure and serve as suggested in step 3.

Per Serving

Macronutrients: 60% Fat, 35% Protein, 5% Carbs

Calories: 376; Total Fat: 25g; Saturated Fat: 13g; Protein: 33g; Total Carbs: 4g; Fiber: 1g; Net Carbs: 3g; Cholesterol: 180mg

Brazilian Fish Stew

DAIRY-FREE, EGG-FREE

Traditionally this fish stew is slow cooked in a terra-cotta casserole, but here we use the slow cooker to make cooking it an absolute breeze. Combining coconut milk and tomatoes with aromatics onion, garlic, ginger, and coriander, this hearty stew is simple to toss together for hands-off cooking. The soup can also be simmered on the stovetop for 2 hours, if you prefer.

Serves 4   **Prep time: 15 minutes / Cook time: 3 hours**

1 pound cod, cut into small pieces
1 tablespoon freshly squeezed lime juice
1 teaspoon grated peeled fresh ginger
3 garlic cloves, minced
2 (14.5-ounce) cans diced tomatoes
1 (13.5-ounce) can coconut milk
¼ cup chopped yellow bell pepper
½ onion, sliced
1 teaspoon red pepper flakes
2 tablespoons chopped fresh cilantro (optional)
4 lime wedges (optional)

1. In a slow cooker, combine the cod, lime juice, ginger, and garlic. Add the tomatoes and their juices, coconut milk, yellow bell pepper, onion, and red pepper flakes.

2. Cover the cooker and cook on low heat for 3 hours, or until the fish flakes easily with a fork.

3. Serve garnished with fresh cilantro (if using) and with lime wedges (if using) for squeezing.

Substitution Tip: If you prefer, shrimp, scallops, or crabmeat can be substituted for the cod.

Instant Pot Tip: Assemble in the Instant Pot as instructed in step 1. Lock the lid in place and seal the vent. Select Manual and cook on High for 10 minutes. After cooking, let the pressure release naturally for 10 minutes. Quick release any remaining pressure and serve as suggested in step 3.

Per Serving

Macronutrients: 49% Fat, 33% Protein, 18% Carbs

Calories: 352; Total Fat: 19g; Saturated Fat: 15g; Protein: 29g; Total Carbs: 12g; Fiber: 2g; Net Carbs: 10g; Cholesterol: 62mg

Creamy Chicken Stew

EGG-FREE

Stews are often thickened with a roux made of flour, which is not allowed in a Paleo diet, and water. For this recipe, almond flour thickens the stew slightly. Although almond flour does not work the same way flour does, it adds substance to the stew without changing the flavor profile. It is not required and can be omitted for a nut-free recipe.

Serves 6   Prep time: 15 minutes / Cook time: 50 minutes

3 tablespoons
  ghee, divided
3 pounds boneless,
  skinless chicken thighs,
  cut into 1-inch cubes
1 teaspoon salt
1 teaspoon freshly
  ground black pepper
1 teaspoon paprika
¼ cup almond flour
4 cups chicken
  broth, divided
2 cups quartered
  radishes
2 carrots, cut
  into chunks
½ cup chopped celery
½ onion, chopped
½ cup coconut cream
  (optional)

1. In a large Dutch oven over medium heat, melt 1½ tablespoons of ghee. Add the chicken, salt, pepper, and paprika. Cook for 10 minutes, stirring occasionally. Using a slotted spoon, remove the chicken and set aside.

2. Add the remaining 1½ tablespoons of ghee to the Dutch oven. Once hot, whisk in the almond flour to combine the fat and flour. Whisk in 1 cup of chicken broth to blend.

3. Add the remaining 3 cups of broth, the radishes, carrots, celery, and onion. Cover the pot and bring the stew to a boil. Reduce the heat to maintain a simmer and cook for 30 minutes.

4. Stir in the coconut cream (if using). Bring the stew back to a simmer, then turn off the heat and serve.

Ingredient Tip: Purchase the chicken precut into cubes to eliminate the process of cutting raw chicken in your kitchen.

Per Serving

Macronutrients: 55% Fat, 38% Protein, 7% Carbs

Calories: 423; Total Fat: 26g; Saturated Fat: 10g; Protein: 40g; Total Carbs: 7g; Fiber: 2g; Net Carbs: 5g; Cholesterol: 228mg

Buffalo Chicken Stew

EGG-FREE, NUT-FREE

Buffalo wings are a tradition for those of us from New York State. However, we don't always want to eat them as an appetizer, so I came up with this stew to change things up a bit. My family enjoys it often and it is a great companion to game-day events. If you're tailgating, this can be transported and kept warm in a slow cooker. This recipe has more than 10 ingredients, but it's one of our family's favorites so it's worth the extra items.

Serves 6   **Prep time: 15 minutes / Cook time: 1 hour**

2 tablespoons ghee

½ cup chopped carrot

¼ cup chopped onion

¼ cup chopped celery

4 garlic cloves, minced

1 pound ground chicken

1 (12-ounce) package frozen cauliflower florets

1 (15-ounce) can diced tomatoes

⅓ cup hot sauce

1 teaspoon paprika

½ teaspoon dried oregano

½ teaspoon ground cumin

1. In a large stockpot over medium-high heat, melt the ghee. Add the carrot, onion, celery, and garlic. Cook for 5 minutes, or until the vegetables are soft.

2. Add the ground chicken and cook for 10 minutes, stirring occasionally to break up the meat, or until lightly browned.

3. Stir in the cauliflower, tomatoes and their juices, hot sauce, paprika, oregano, and cumin. Bring the stew to a boil. Lower the heat to maintain a simmer and cook for 40 minutes until sauce reduces and thickens.

Option Tip: Serve this stew over cauliflower rice.

Per Serving

Macronutrients: 53% Fat, 36% Protein, 11% Carbs

Calories: 220; Total Fat: 13g; Saturated Fat: 5g; Protein: 20g; Total Carbs: 8g; Fiber: 3g; Net Carbs: 5g; Cholesterol: 92mg

Pork Stew

This stew is rich in flavor with a comfort food feel thanks to the pork, mushrooms, and the creamy broth. Save time peeling and mincing garlic by buying a jar of already-minced garlic to keep in your refrigerator. One teaspoon of minced garlic equals one medium clove.

Serves 4   Prep time: 10 minutes / Cook time: 4 to 6 hours

2 cups chicken
  bone broth
8 ounces
  mushrooms, sliced
1 small onion, chopped
5 garlic cloves, minced
1 tablespoon coconut oil
2 teaspoons
  dried oregano
2 teaspoons dried
  mustard
1 pound pork loin, cut
  into ½-inch cubes
¼ cup coconut milk

1. In a slow cooker, stir together the chicken bone broth, mushrooms, onion, garlic, coconut oil, oregano, and mustard.

2. Stir in the pork.

3. Cover the cooker and cook on low heat for 4 to 6 hours.

4. Stir in the coconut milk. Adjust the slow cooker setting to high heat and cook, uncovered, for 15 minutes.

Instant Pot Tip: Select the Sauté setting and add the coconut oil to melt. Add the pork loin and cook for about 3 minutes, browning it on all sides. Add the remaining ingredients. Lock the lid in place and seal the vent. Select Manual, and cook on High for 25 minutes. After cooking, quick release the pressure. Carefully unlock and remove the lid. Stir in the coconut milk. Select Sauté again and simmer for 15 minutes before serving.

Per Serving

Macronutrients: 46% Fat, 45% Protein, 9% Carbs

Calories: 335; Total Fat: 17g; Saturated Fat: 8g; Protein: 38g; Total Carbs: 6g; Fiber: 1g; Net Carbs: 5g; Cholesterol: 95mg

Beef and Butternut Stew

EGG-FREE, NUT-FREE

Butternut squash is a good source of vitamin A, potassium, and fiber. Beef provides a large amount of nutrition in a small serving that is high in protein, B vitamins, and zinc. The ingredients in this stew give it a sweet, warm heat.

Serves 8   **Prep time: 15 minutes / Cook time: 1 hour, 25 minutes**

1½ pounds ground beef
1 tablespoon ghee
1 small onion,
   finely chopped
½ cup chopped green
   bell pepper
2 tablespoons
   tomato paste
4 garlic cloves, minced
1 jalapeño
   pepper, chopped
⅔ cup beef broth
1 teaspoon ground cumin
¼ teaspoon ground
   cinnamon
1 (28-ounce) can diced
   tomatoes
2 cups chopped peeled
   butternut squash
2 carrots, chopped
1 tablespoon maple syrup
Chopped fresh cilantro,
   for garnish (optional)

1. Heat a large Dutch oven over medium-high heat. Add the ground beef and sauté for 8 minutes, stirring occasionally to break up the meat, or until the beef is browned. Remove from the Dutch oven and set aside. Wipe the Dutch oven clean with a paper towel.

2. Return the Dutch oven to the heat and add the ghee to melt. Add the onion and green bell pepper. Sauté for 3 minutes, or until the onion is translucent.

3. Stir in the tomato paste, garlic, and jalapeño. Sauté for 2 minutes, stirring constantly.

4. Stir in the beef broth to deglaze the pan, stirring to scrape up any browned bits from the bottom. Bring the broth to a boil and cook for 2 minutes.

5. Return the ground beef to the Dutch oven. Stir in the cumin and cinnamon. Add the tomatoes and their juices, butternut squash, carrots, and maple syrup.

CONTINUED

Beef and Butternut Stew, CONTINUED

6. Bring the stew to a boil. Reduce the heat to maintain a simmer and cook for 1 hour, or until the vegetables are tender.

7. Garnish with fresh cilantro (if using) to serve.

Substitution Tip: Honey or sugar-free syrup can be substituted for the maple syrup without changing the flavor of this recipe. Sometimes I like just a little more sweet to counteract the heat and will add another ½ to 1 tablespoon of sweetener.

Per Serving

Macronutrients: 58% Fat, 22% Protein, 20% Carbs

Calories: 310; Total Fat: 20g; Saturated Fat: 8g; Protein: 17g; Total Carbs: 17g; Fiber: 4g; Net Carbs: 13g; Cholesterol: 68mg

Chipotle Beef and Sweet Potato Stew

DAIRY-FREE, EGG-FREE, NUT-FREE

My favorite combination of flavors is smoky sweet heat. The chipotle and sweet potato bring those flavors together, making this one of my favorite recipes. If you wish to thicken this stew, when it is done cooking, mix 1 teaspoon arrowroot powder with 1 tablespoon of water. Turn the slow cooker to high heat and stir the mixture into the stew, then cook for 15 minutes more.

Serves 6　**Prep time: 15 minutes / Cook time: 4 to 6 hours**

1 (14.5-ounce) can diced tomatoes

1 cup beef broth

1 tablespoon chili powder

1½ teaspoons cocoa powder

½ teaspoon salt

¼ teaspoon freshly ground black pepper

1 canned chipotle pepper in adobo sauce, minced

1 tablespoon erythritol, or honey (optional)

1 pound beef stew meat

1 cup peeled chopped sweet potato

1. In a slow cooker, whisk the tomatoes and their juices, beef broth, chili powder, cocoa powder, salt, pepper, chipotle pepper, and erythritol (if using).

2. Stir in the stew meat and sweet potato.

3. Cover the cooker and cook on low heat for 4 to 6 hours.

Instant Pot Tip: Select the Sauté setting and add 1 tablespoon avocado oil to heat. Add the stew meat and brown on all sides, 5 to 10 minutes. Add the remaining ingredients. Lock the lid in place and seal the vent. Select Manual and cook on High for 30 minutes. After cooking, let the pressure release naturally for 30 minutes, then quick release any remaining pressure.

Per Serving

Macronutrients: 38% Fat, 42% Protein, 20% Carbs

Calories: 156; Total Fat: 5g; Saturated Fat: 1g; Protein: 18g; Total Carbs: 9g; Fiber: 2g; Net Carbs: 7g; Cholesterol: 51mg

Curry Roasted Cauliflower, page 77

Chapter Four

VEGETABLE MAINS

Chopped Veggie Salad Bowl

DAIRY-FREE, EGG-FREE, MEATLESS, NUT-FREE

This chopped veggie salad is a bowlful of vitamins B, C, and K as well as a good source of fiber. I often bring this delicious veggie bowl when we are invited to summer picnics but it makes a tasty addition to your table year-round. It can be enjoyed as a whole meal on its own or served as a side dish. I like to serve it with Sheet Pan Fish and Chips (page 93).

Serves 8　**Prep time: 10 minutes**

½ cup extra-virgin olive oil

¼ cup freshly squeezed lemon juice

2 teaspoons salt

1 teaspoon dried basil

½ teaspoon dried oregano

¼ teaspoon ground cumin

½ head red cabbage, roughly chopped

½ head green cabbage, roughly chopped

1 large carrot, shredded

3 scallions, white and green parts, sliced

1. In a large bowl, whisk the olive oil, lemon juice, salt, basil, oregano, and cumin to blend.

2. Add the red and green cabbage, carrot, and scallions to the bowl. Toss to coat.

Option Tip: To cut carbs from this recipe, remove the carrot from the ingredients.

Per Serving

Macronutrients: 78% Fat, 5% Protein, 17% Carbs

Calories: 162; Total Fat: 14g; Saturated Fat: 2g; Protein: 2g; Total Carbs: 11g; Fiber: 3g; Net Carbs: 8g; Cholesterol: 0mg

Zucchini Noodles with Avocado Pesto

DAIRY-FREE, EGG-FREE, MEATLESS

Avocado fans will love this recipe. It is packed with good-for-you fat and fiber and makes a delicious summer side to a grilled steak. The zucchini noodles in this recipe are coated with a creamy flavorful "pesto" made with the avocado. This raw dish has a crisp bite complemented by the creamy lightly spiced sauce.

Serves 6   Prep time: 10 minutes

1 avocado, peeled, halved, and pitted

1 cup fresh basil leaves

¼ cup raw cashews

1 garlic clove, minced

1 tablespoon freshly squeezed lemon juice

1 tablespoon avocado oil

1 teaspoon ground cumin

3 zucchini, spiralized, long strands cut into shorter noodles

1. In a food processor, combine the avocado, basil, cashews, garlic, lemon juice, avocado oil, and cumin. Process until smooth. If the sauce is too thick, add 1 tablespoon of water at a time until the sauce is the consistency you like.

2. Divide the zucchini noodles between 4 serving bowls. Pour the avocado pesto over the noodles and toss to coat.

Ingredient Tip: Soak the cashews in ½ cup hot water for 2 hours before making the avocado sauce. Doing so softens the cashews and makes the sauce even creamier. This is not required but produces a smoother sauce.

Per Serving

Macronutrients: 69% Fat, 10% Protein, 21% Carbs

Calories: 118; Total Fat: 9g; Saturated Fat: 1g; Protein: 3g; Total Carbs: 8g; Fiber: 4g; Net Carbs: 4g; Cholesterol: 0mg

Spicy Asian-Style Zoodle Bowl

DAIRY-FREE, EGG-FREE, MEATLESS

I am a huge fan of the sweet and spicy combination. The sweetness from the honey blends well with the hot chili sauce and tames the heat. I love how the sauce coats the vegetables and blends with the different flavors and texture of each. This bowl is delicious anytime, but makes a great summertime picnic salad.

Serves 4   **Prep time: 15 minutes**

¼ cup almond butter

2 tablespoons coconut aminos

1 teaspoon hot chili sauce

1 teaspoon erythritol or honey

¼ teaspoon salt

2 zucchini, spiralized

1 cup sliced radishes

1 cup chopped kale

2 tablespoons chopped almonds

1. In a large bowl, whisk the almond butter, coconut aminos, chili sauce, erythritol, and salt to blend.

2. Add the zucchini, radishes, and kale to the bowl. Toss to coat the vegetables with the sauce.

3. Garnish with almonds and serve.

Ingredient Tip: To add a variety of colors to this salad, look for multicolored radishes. When sliced, the color on the outside of the radish is also in the core and is very appealing to the eye.

Per Serving

Macronutrients: 65% Fat, 13% Protein, 22% Carbs

Calories: 153; Total Fat: 11g; Saturated Fat: 1g; Protein: 5g; Total Carbs: 12g; Fiber: 4g; Net Carbs: 8g; Cholesterol: 0mg

Cabbage Carrot Salad with Sesame Ginger Dressing

DAIRY-FREE, EGG-FREE, MEATLESS, NUT-FREE

Ginger is considered a powerful antioxidant with an anti-inflammatory effect that may help reduce muscle pain. It contributes to the delicious flavors in the salad dressing. This is one of those salads that's better in the days after you make it when it has had time to sit and the sauce soaks into the vegetables. It is super easy to make and has a lighter taste and feel to it than a traditional mayonnaise-based salad.

Serves 6   **Prep time: 15 minutes**

2 tablespoons
  coconut aminos
2 tablespoons sesame oil
2 garlic cloves, minced
1½ teaspoons minced
  peeled fresh ginger
1 teaspoon sesame seeds
1 teaspoon salt
½ teaspoon freshly
  ground black pepper
½ teaspoon red
  pepper flakes
½ head cabbage,
  shredded
2 large carrots, shredded
½ cup sunflower seeds

1. In a large bowl, whisk the coconut aminos, sesame oil, garlic, ginger, sesame seeds, salt, pepper, and red pepper flakes to blend.

2. Add the cabbage, carrots, and sunflower seeds to the bowl and toss to coat with the dressing.

Ingredient Tip: If you like a little bit of sweet in your slaw, add 1 or 2 teaspoons honey to the dressing.

Per Serving

Macronutrients: 69% Fat, 9% Protein, 22% Carbs

Calories: 131; Total Fat: 10g; Saturated Fat: 1g; Protein: 3g; Total Carbs: 9g; Fiber: 3g; Net Carbs: 6g; Cholesterol: 0mg

Cauliflower Fried Rice

DAIRY-FREE, EGG-FREE, MEATLESS, NUT-FREE

Cauliflower fried rice goes so well with so many dishes. I use it in the same way many people use rice as a side dish. This is a great recipe to have on hand; it is versatile—toss it with scrambled eggs, cooked chicken, or chopped ham to make a heartier dish.

Serves 6   **Prep time: 10 minutes / Cook time: 15 minutes**

1 tablespoon sesame oil
½ small onion, chopped
½ cup chopped carrot
1 head cauliflower, finely chopped
2 tablespoons coconut aminos
1 teaspoon salt
2 small scallions, white and green parts, sliced

1. In a large skillet over medium heat, heat the sesame oil. Add the onion and carrot and sauté for 3 minutes, or until the onion is translucent.

2. Stir in the cauliflower. Cover the skillet and cook for 6 minutes, stirring frequently, until the cauliflower starts to turn opaque.

3. Stir in the coconut aminos and salt. Cook for 5 minutes more, until the cauliflower is tender but not mushy.

4. Remove from the heat and stir in the scallions to serve.

Cooking Tip: Watch the cauliflower carefully as it cooks. If cauliflower overcooks, it becomes mushy and unappetizing. To get the best results, the cauliflower rice should still be slightly firm with a slight bite.

Per Serving

Macronutrients: 44% Fat, 13% Protein, 43% Carbs

Calories: 61; Total Fat: 3g; Saturated Fat: 1g; Protein: 2g; Total Carbs: 9g; Fiber: 3g; Net Carbs: 6g; Cholesterol: 0mg

Cauliflower Rice Tabbouleh

DAIRY-FREE, EGG-FREE, MEATLESS, NUT-FREE

Tabbouleh normally includes bulgur as an ingredient. However, bulgur is a grain, which isn't part of a Paleo diet and lifestyle. In my version, cauliflower rice takes the place of bulgur. Even though it's not as absorbent, it still has a wonderful flavor. The key is to let the dish sit for a bit so the flavors blend before you serve it.

Serves 6   Prep time: 15 minutes, plus chilling time

1 head cauliflower, riced

2 cups sliced English
  cucumber

2 cups chopped cherry
  tomatoes

1 cup chopped
  fresh parsley

1 cup chopped fresh mint

¼ cup freshly squeezed
  lemon juice

¼ cup extra-virgin
  olive oil

4 scallions, white and
  green parts, minced

2 teaspoons salt

1. In a large bowl, stir together the cauliflower, cucumber, tomatoes, parsley, mint, lemon juice, olive oil, scallions, and salt.

2. Refrigerate for 30 minutes before serving.

Option Tip: Serve over a bed of shredded romaine lettuce with slices of grilled chicken breast on the side.

Per Serving

Macronutrients: 66% Fat, 9% Protein, 25% Carbs

Calories: 136; Total Fat: 10g; Saturated Fat: 1g;
Protein: 3g; Total Carbs: 13g; Fiber: 4g; Net Carbs: 9g;
Cholesterol: 0mg

Mediterranean Cauliflower Salad

DAIRY-FREE, EGG-FREE, MEATLESS, NUT-FREE

Feta cheese is a mainstay in Mediterranean dishes—salad or otherwise. But cheese isn't part of a Paleo diet and you won't find it here. Omitting that ingredient doesn't mean I've skimped on flavor. Instead, briny kalamata olives give this salad that familiar salty flavor.

Serves 6   Prep time: 15 minutes

½ cup extra-virgin
  olive oil
¼ cup freshly squeezed
  lemon juice
2 teaspoons salt
1 teaspoon dried basil
½ teaspoon
  dried oregano
¼ teaspoon
  ground cumin
1 head
  cauliflower, chopped
2 cups grape
  tomatoes, halved
1 green bell
  pepper, chopped
1 English
  cucumber, chopped
½ cup pitted halved
  kalamata olives
½ small red onion,
  finely chopped

1. In a large bowl, whisk the olive oil, lemon juice, salt, basil, oregano, and cumin to blend.

2. Add the cauliflower, tomatoes, green bell pepper, cucumber, olives, and red onion to the bowl and toss to coat.

3. Cover and refrigerate until ready to serve.

Ingredient Tip: Make the salad dressing ahead of time so the flavors have time to blend.

Per Serving

Macronutrients: 81% Fat, 5% Protein, 14% Carbs

Calories: 243; Total Fat: 22g; Saturated Fat: 3g; Protein: 3g; Total Carbs: 12g; Fiber: 4g; Net Carbs: 8g; Cholesterol: 0mg

Curry Roasted Cauliflower

EGG-FREE, MEATLESS, NUT-FREE

Roasting vegetables brings out a tremendous amount of their flavor. By tossing the cauliflower with ghee and spices before roasting, you add many other levels of flavor to this normally bland vegetable. The caramelization of the roasted cauliflower adds a slightly sweet taste that, when combined with the spices, makes this a very appealing meal.

Serves 4   **Prep time: 10 minutes / Cook time: 30 minutes**

1 head cauliflower, cut
  into florets
2 tablespoons
  ghee, melted
2 tablespoons yellow
  curry powder
1 teaspoon ground
  turmeric
1 teaspoon salt
½ teaspoon
  garlic powder
½ teaspoon
  onion powder
½ cup chopped fresh
  cilantro

1. Preheat the oven to 400°F.

2. In a large bowl, toss together the cauliflower, ghee, curry powder, turmeric, salt, garlic powder, and onion powder. Transfer to a sheet pan.

3. Roast for 30 minutes, or until some of the cauliflower is browned and crispy.

4. Remove from the oven and sprinkle with cilantro to serve.

Option Tip: For a more buttery flavor, drizzle 1 tablespoon melted ghee over the cauliflower when tossing with the cilantro.

Per Serving

Macronutrients: 61% Fat, 14% Protein, 25% Carbs

Calories: 118; Total Fat: 8g; Saturated Fat: 5g;
Protein: 4g; Total Carbs: 11g; Fiber: 5g; Net Carbs: 6g;
Cholesterol: 15mg

Cabbage Noodles

DAIRY-FREE, EGG-FREE, MEATLESS

There is a dish at a restaurant in my hometown made with cabbage and egg noodles. That dish is off limits since our diet changed, but I miss it. So, I created this recipe to replicate the dish. Cabbage noodles are meant to be a main course, so the servings are large. The portions can be cut down and served as a side dish to chicken or pork. Bacon also goes really well in this dish, if you want to boost the protein and fats.

Serves 4 **Prep time: 15 minutes / Cook time: 25 minutes**

2 tablespoons avocado oil
½ cup sliced onion
2 garlic cloves, minced
2 cups sliced mushrooms
½ cup sliced carrot
8 cups shredded cabbage
¼ teaspoon red pepper flakes
1 teaspoon salt
½ teaspoon freshly ground black pepper
Coconut aminos, for garnish (optional)

1. In a large skillet over medium-high heat, heat the avocado oil. Add the onion and garlic. Sauté for 3 to 5 minutes until translucent.

2. Add the mushrooms and sauté for 5 minutes, or until their water has released. Stir in the carrot and sauté for about 3 minutes until the carrot starts to soften.

3. Add the cabbage, red pepper flakes, salt, and pepper. Stir-fry for 10 minutes until the cabbage is crisp-tender and caramelized. Season with coconut aminos (if using).

Substitution Tip: This recipe takes well to vegetable substitutes. Feel free to substitute any of the vegetables with broccoli, cauliflower, spinach, or zucchini.

Per Serving

Macronutrients: 46% Fat, 12% Protein, 42% Carbs

Calories: 136; Total Fat: 7g; Saturated Fat: 1g; Protein: 4g; Total Carbs: 14g; Fiber: 6g; Net Carbs: 8g; Cholesterol: 0mg

Vegetable Lo Mein

EGG-FREE, MEATLESS

If you're missing takeout lo mein noodles, this vegetable lo mein made with zucchini noodles can help you resist temptation. Spiralized zucchini noodles can be very long. To make it easier to serve, chop the noodles so they are no more than 4 inches long. You'll also see that the shorter noodles translate to a shorter cook time, too.

Serves 4   **Prep time: 10 minutes / Cook time: 10 minutes**

1 tablespoon ghee

2 cups sliced mushrooms

½ red bell pepper, julienned

1 carrot, julienned

2 scallions, white and green parts, sliced, divided

2 garlic cloves, minced

2 zucchini, spiralized

2 tablespoons coconut aminos

1 teaspoon sesame oil

1 teaspoon honey (optional)

1. In a large skillet over medium heat, melt the ghee. Add the mushrooms, red bell pepper, carrot, white scallion parts, and garlic. Sauté for 7 minutes, or until the carrot is fork-tender.

2. Stir in the zucchini noodles, coconut aminos, sesame oil, and honey (if using), stirring to coat. Cook for 1 minute, or until the noodles are at your desired level of softness.

3. Garnish with the green scallion parts and serve.

   Substitution Tip: Eliminate the honey and add an equal amount of erythritol instead, if desired.

> **Per Serving**
>
> **Macronutrients: 51% Fat, 14% Protein, 35% Carbs**
>
> Calories: 88; Total Fat: 5g; Saturated Fat: 3g; Protein: 3g; Total Carbs: 9g; Fiber: 2g; Net Carbs: 7g; Cholesterol: 8mg

Pasta Primavera with Veggie Noodles

EGG-FREE, MEATLESS, NUT-FREE

To brighten this recipe, a combination of zucchini, yellow squash, carrots, and asparagus is used to make the "noodle" portion of the dish. Cut the asparagus into thin, pasta-like slices. Depending on the cut of asparagus, the number of "noodles" to cut will vary. Because cheese is not allowed in a Paleo diet, a ghee and garlic sauce coats the noodles for a zesty buttery flavor.

Serves 4   **Prep time: 10 minutes / Cook time: 10 minutes**

2 tablespoons
  ghee, divided
4 garlic cloves, minced
2 tablespoons freshly
  squeezed lemon juice
1 teaspoon Italian
  seasoning
2 cups zucchini noodles
2 cups yellow
  squash noodles
2 carrots, spiralized
1 cup butternut
  squash noodles
10 asparagus stalks, very
  thinly sliced lengthwise
1 cup arugula
Salt
Freshly ground
  black pepper

1. In a large skillet over medium heat, melt 1 tablespoon of ghee. Stir in the garlic, lemon juice, and Italian seasoning. Simmer for 1 minute.

2. Add the remaining 1 tablespoon of ghee and the zucchini, yellow squash, carrot, and butternut squash noodles and the asparagus and arugula. Toss the veggie noodles and arugula with the sauce. Cook for 7 minutes, or until the veggie noodles are tender.

3. Taste and season with salt and pepper.

Substitution Tip: Reduce the carbs by eliminating the butternut squash and carrot and increasing the zucchini and yellow squash to 3 cups each.

Per Serving

Macronutrients: 43% Fat, 11% Protein, 46% Carbs

Calories: 147; Total Fat: 7g; Saturated Fat: 4g; Protein: 4g; Total Carbs: 21g; Fiber: 7g; Net Carbs: 14g; Cholesterol: 16mg

Thai-Style Butternut Squash

DAIRY-FREE, EGG-FREE

This Thai-style curry is a big bowl of satisfying comfort food. If you like Thai flavors, this sweet and spicy dish will be just what you need to warm your heart and soul. I like to cut the cabbage into medium strips to allow for the effect of having a "noodle" in the recipe.

Serves 4   Prep time: 15 minutes / Cook time: 25 minutes

1 tablespoon coconut oil

2 cups chopped peeled
  butternut squash

1 cup sliced
  napa cabbage

3 garlic cloves, minced

1 (13.5-ounce) can
  coconut milk

2 tablespoons
  almond butter

2 tablespoons red
  curry paste

1 teaspoon fish sauce

1 tablespoon freshly
  squeezed lime juice

1 tablespoon honey

½ cup sliced almonds
  (optional)

1. In a large skillet over medium heat, melt the coconut oil. Stir in the butternut squash and cook for 7 minutes, or until the squash just begins to soften.

2. Add the cabbage and garlic and stir-fry for 3 minutes, or until the cabbage begins to wilt. Remove the squash and cabbage mixture from the skillet and set aside.

3. Return the skillet to the heat and add the coconut milk, almond butter, curry paste, fish sauce, lime juice, and honey. Whisk to combine. Bring the broth to a boil.

4. Return the squash mixture to the skillet. Turn the heat to low and simmer for 10 minutes, or until the squash is cooked through and sauce begins to thicken.

5. Serve topped with sliced almonds (if using).

Ingredient Tip: Whole butternut squash comes in many different sizes. The average squash can weigh between 2 and 4 pounds. A 3-pound squash yields about 4 cups of chopped squash.

Per Serving

Macronutrients: 72% Fat, 5% Protein, 23% Carbs

Calories: 327; Total Fat: 26g; Saturated Fat: 18g;
Protein: 4g; Total Carbs: 22g; Fiber: 4g; Net Carbs: 18g;
Cholesterol: 0mg

Roasted Portobello Mushroom Tacos

DAIRY-FREE, EGG-FREE, MEATLESS, NUT-FREE

Portobello mushrooms are large caps that are thick and sturdy. When cooked, they have a chewy, meaty texture. Roasting the portobello mushrooms creates a caramelization with a delicious earthy flavor.

Serves 4   **Prep time: 10 minutes / Cook time: 12 minutes**

---

4 large portobello mushroom caps, sliced

1 small onion, sliced

1 tablespoon extra-virgin olive oil

1 tablespoon chili powder

1 teaspoon ground cumin

1 teaspoon salt

8 romaine lettuce leaves

1 avocado, peeled, halved, pitted, and sliced

½ cup salsa (optional)

2 tablespoons chopped fresh cilantro

1. Preheat the oven to 375°F.

2. On a sheet pan, combine the mushrooms, onion, olive oil, chili powder, cumin, and salt. Stir to coat.

3. Roast, stirring occasionally, for 12 minutes, or until the mushrooms begin to brown and the onion is cooked.

4. Serve the mushrooms in romaine lettuce leaves topped with avocado, salsa (if using), and cilantro.

Substitution Tip: Substitute an egg wrap for the romaine leaf to boost the protein in this recipe. Just whisk 1 egg per wrap and cook it in a hot skillet, flipping to cook both sides. Let cool before wrapping the taco filling inside the egg wrap. To make this quicker, you can make several egg wraps ahead and refrigerate them until ready to use.

Per Serving

Macronutrients: 58% Fat, 14% Protein, 28% Carbs

Calories: 140; Total Fat: 9g; Saturated Fat: 1g; Protein: 5g; Total Carbs: 13g; Fiber: 5g; Net Carbs: 8g; Cholesterol: 0mg

Portobello Mushroom Pizzas

DAIRY-FREE, EGG-FREE, MEATLESS, NUT-FREE

Nutritional yeast flakes are rich in B vitamins and lend a cheesy flavor to a dish. Because Paleo restricts cheese, nutritional yeast flakes and Paleo-friendly mayonnaise are combined in this recipe to add a level of cheesy flavor to the pizza. Although it will not melt like cheese, it will still have a savory delicious flavor that satisfies.

Serves 4   Prep time: 10 minutes / Cook time: 20 minutes

½ cup Paleo-friendly (egg-free) mayonnaise

¼ cup nutritional yeast flakes

4 large portobello mushrooms, stemmed and gills removed

1 tablespoon extra-virgin olive oil

¼ cup tomato sauce

½ cup chopped artichoke hearts

¼ cup sliced cherry tomatoes

2 tablespoons sliced black olives

¼ cup torn arugula

1. Preheat the oven to 400°F.

2. In a small bowl, stir together the mayonnaise and nutritional yeast flakes until combined.

3. Brush each mushroom with olive oil and place the mushrooms, stem-side up, on a sheet pan.

4. Evenly spread the mayonnaise mixture on the inside of each mushroom cap and repeat with the tomato sauce.

5. Evenly top each mushroom with artichoke hearts, cherry tomatoes, and black olives.

6. Bake for 20 minutes.

7. Add the arugula to the pizzas after baking.

Ingredient Tip: Clean the portobello mushrooms by gently brushing them with a damp paper towel to remove any dirt. Remove the stem from each mushroom and use a spoon to scoop out the gills.

Per Serving

Macronutrients: 86% Fat, 12% Protein, 2% Carbs

Calories: 304; Total Fat: 29g; Saturated Fat: 4g; Protein: 9g; Total Carbs: 10g; Fiber: 4g; Net Carbs: 6g; Cholesterol: 30mg

Skillet Ratatouille

DAIRY-FREE, EGG-FREE, MEATLESS, NUT-FREE

This recipe has a higher carb count than most, so keep portion sizes in mind. The vegetables are seasoned with fragrant oregano, basil, thyme, and fennel, lending an Italian feel to this comfort food.

Serves 6 to 8   **Prep time: 15 minutes / Cook time: 30 minutes**

4 tablespoons
  extra-virgin olive
  oil, divided
1 small onion, chopped
½ cup chopped yellow
  bell pepper
2 garlic cloves, minced
1 eggplant, chopped
1 small zucchini, chopped
4 large
  tomatoes, chopped
1 teaspoon honey
1 teaspoon salt
½ teaspoon red
  pepper flakes
½ teaspoon
  dried oregano
¼ teaspoon dried thyme
¼ teaspoon fennel seeds
½ cup shredded fresh
  basil leaves

1. In a large cast iron skillet, heat 1 tablespoon of olive oil over medium heat. Add the onion, yellow bell pepper, and garlic. Cook for 3 minutes, or until softened.

2. Warm 1 tablespoon of olive oil in the skillet. Mix in the eggplant and cook for 10 minutes, or until the eggplant is soft. Transfer the vegetables to a plate and set aside.

3. Return the skillet to the heat and add the remaining 2 tablespoons of olive oil along with the zucchini. Cook for 5 minutes, or until crisp-tender.

4. Stir in the tomatoes, honey, salt, red pepper flakes, oregano, thyme, and fennel seeds.

5. Return the vegetables to the skillet and stir to combine. Bring to a boil, then reduce the heat to maintain a simmer. Cook for 12 minutes.

6. Serve topped with basil.

Substitution Tip: I like to use a cast iron skillet for this recipe because it holds heat and heats evenly. However, if you do not have a cast iron skillet, a regular skillet will work.

Per Serving

Macronutrients: 63% Fat, 6% Protein, 31% Carbs

Calories: 142; Total Fat: 10g; Saturated Fat: 1g; Protein: 2g; Total Carbs: 15g; Fiber: 4g; Net Carbs: 11g; Cholesterol: 0mg

Sweet Potato Pad Thai

DAIRY-FREE, EGG-FREE

Pad thai gets a lower-carb makeover in this recipe that uses sweet potato noodles in place of the traditional rice noodles. Coated with a sweet and spicy nut sauce and garnished with lime, cilantro, and chopped almonds, this better-than-takeout recipe is ready in just 30 minutes.

Serves 4   **Prep time: 10 minutes / Cook time: 20 minutes**

For the almond sauce

2 tablespoons almond butter

3 tablespoons chicken broth

1½ tablespoons coconut aminos

1 teaspoon honey

1 teaspoon sesame oil

1 teaspoon red pepper flakes

¼ teaspoon ground ginger

For the pad thai

1 tablespoon extra-virgin olive oil

2 sweet potatoes, spiralized

Salt

Freshly ground black pepper

¼ cup chicken broth

¼ cup chopped fresh cilantro

2 tablespoons chopped almonds

To make the almond sauce

In a small bowl, whisk the almond butter, chicken broth, coconut aminos, honey, sesame oil, red pepper flakes, and ginger until smooth. Set aside.

To make the pad thai

1. In a large skillet over medium heat, heat the olive oil. Add the sweet potato noodles and season with salt and pepper. Sauté for 5 minutes, stirring occasionally.

2. Add the chicken broth and sauté for 5 minutes more, or until the noodles are crisp-tender.

3. Pour the almond sauce over the noodles and toss to coat. Cook for 2 minutes to heat the sauce.

4. Serve topped with cilantro and almonds.

Ingredient Tip: Any kind of nut butter (with the exception of peanut) can be substituted in the almond sauce. Look for all-natural nut butter made only with nuts and/or salt.

Per Serving

Macronutrients: 52% Fat, 6% Protein, 42% Carbs

Calories: 191; Total Fat: 11g; Saturated Fat: 1g; Protein: 3g; Total Carbs: 21g; Fiber: 3g; Net Carbs: 18g; Cholesterol: 1mg

Sweet Potato Curry

DAIRY-FREE, EGG-FREE, MEATLESS

Sweet potatoes and spinach are packed with vitamins, antioxidants, and fiber. Spinach is high in vitamins A, K, and B, to name a few. It is great for healthy bones and joints. Sweet potatoes are packed with B and C vitamins and are good for eye and skin health as well as the immune system. This simple, delicious curry is loaded with both vegetables. Its creamy, savory, and sweet flavors are a delight.

Serves 6   **Prep time: 10 minutes / Cook time: 30 minutes**

1 tablespoon extra-virgin
   olive oil
1 small shallot, chopped
2 sweet
   potatoes, chopped
Salt
Freshly ground
   black pepper
1 (13.5-ounce) can full-fat
   coconut milk
½ cup water
3 tablespoons red
   curry paste
2 tablespoons freshly
   squeezed lime juice
5 cups fresh
   baby spinach

1. In a large skillet over medium heat, heat the olive oil until hot. Add the shallot and cook for 2 minutes, or until the shallot begins to look translucent.

2. Add the sweet potatoes to the skillet and toss with the shallot. Season with salt and pepper. Cook for 15 minutes, stirring occasionally.

3. In a medium bowl, whisk the coconut milk, ½ cup water, curry paste, and lime juice to combine. Add the sauce to the potatoes and stir to coat. Simmer the potatoes for 10 minutes, or until they are soft.

4. Stir in the baby spinach and cook for 2 minutes.

Option Tip: This curry is delicious over steamed cauliflower. Buy the cauliflower you steam right in the bag and cook it 5 minutes before serving time.

Per Serving

Macronutrients: 61% Fat, 6% Protein, 33% Carbs

Calories: 205; Total Fat: 14g; Saturated Fat: 10g; Protein: 3g; Total Carbs: 16g; Fiber: 2g; Net Carbs: 14g; Cholesterol: 0mg

Stuffed Acorn Squash

EGG-FREE, MEATLESS

Stuffed with walnuts, apple, and cranberries, this fall favorite is deliciously savory and sweet as well as filling. Cooking time will vary depending on the size of the squash. The squash is cooked through when you can squeeze the top and it is soft, or when you can easily pierce it with a fork.

Serves 4   **Prep time: 10 minutes / Cook time: 35 minutes**

2 acorn squash, halved and seeded

¼ cup maple syrup

6 teaspoons ghee, divided

1 teaspoon salt

½ teaspoon freshly ground black pepper

1 cup chopped walnuts

1 apple, chopped

½ cup chopped cranberries

1 tablespoon minced fresh sage leaves

1. Preheat the oven to 425°F.

2. Place the acorn squash, cut-side up, on a large sheet pan. Place 1 tablespoon of maple syrup and 1½ teaspoons of ghee in each squash half. Season with salt and pepper.

3. Roast the squash for 20 minutes.

4. In a small bowl, toss together the walnuts, apple, cranberries, and sage.

5. Remove the squash from the oven and evenly divide the walnut mixture among the squash halves.

6. Bake for 15 minutes more, or until the tops of the squash feel soft when you press them.

7. If desired, remove the squash from the shell and combine the squash and filling before serving.

Substitution Tip: Substitute pear and chopped fresh thyme for the apple and sage for a flavor twist.

Per Serving

Macronutrients: 56% Fat, 6% Protein, 38% Carbs

Calories: 415; Total Fat: 26g; Saturated Fat: 6g; Protein: 6g; Total Carbs: 47g; Fiber: 10g; Net Carbs: 37g; Cholesterol: 16mg

Jalapeño Shrimp and "Grits," page 98

Chapter Five

SEAFOOD AND SHELLFISH

Garlic Roasted Cod

EGG-FREE

Almond meal is a coarser grind of almond than almond flour and is used in this recipe to give more texture to the fish topping. You can change the flavor profile of this recipe and substitute chili powder or Italian seasoning for the parsley.

Serves 4   **Prep time: 10 minutes / Cook time: 10 minutes**

For the topping

¼ cup ghee

2 tablespoons freshly
   squeezed lemon juice

1 large garlic
   clove, minced

1 tablespoon chopped
   fresh parsley

1 tablespoon
   almond meal

2 teaspoons
   minced shallot

Salt

Freshly ground
   black pepper

For the fish

1½ teaspoons ghee

4 (6-ounce) cod fillets

¼ teaspoon salt

¼ teaspoon
   ground cumin

¼ teaspoon
   cayenne pepper

To make the topping

In a bowl, stir together the ghee, lemon juice, garlic, parsley, almond meal, and shallot. Season with salt and pepper. Set aside.

To make the fish

1. Preheat the oven to 450°F.

2. In a large oven-safe skillet over medium-high heat, melt the ghee. Place the fish in the skillet and sprinkle evenly with salt, cumin, and cayenne. Cook the fish for 4 minutes, flip the fish, and cook for 1 minute more.

3. Evenly divide the topping over the fish and transfer the skillet to the oven.

4. Bake the fish for 3 minutes, or until it flakes easily with a fork. Spoon the ghee in the pan over the fish before serving.

Cooking Tip: An oven-safe nonstick skillet is best to use when making this recipe. Fish tends to stick, and using cast iron or a skillet without a nonstick coating can cause the fish to stick and fall apart in the skillet.

Per Serving

Macronutrients: 48% Fat, 46% Protein, 6% Carbs

Calories: 340; Total Fat: 18g; Saturated Fat: 10g; Protein: 39g; Total Carbs: 2g; Fiber: 0g; Net Carbs: 2g; Cholesterol: 127mg

Lemon Garlic Sheet Pan Salmon

EGG-FREE, NUT-FREE

Salmon is a great choice to enjoy in a Paleo diet. It is a nutrient-rich fish also rich in omega-3 fatty acids, and good for eye health, brain health, and heart health. In the last step, the maple and lemon caramelize, giving the salmon a rich flavor.

Serves 4   Prep time: 10 minutes / Cook time: 23 minutes

1 lemon, sliced

1½ pounds skin-on
    salmon fillet

⅓ cup ghee, melted

2 tablespoons freshly
    squeezed lemon juice

1 tablespoon maple syrup

4 large garlic
    cloves, minced

1 teaspoon salt

½ teaspoon freshly
    ground black pepper

½ teaspoon paprika

1 tablespoon chopped
    fresh chives (optional)

1. Preheat the oven to 375°F. Line a sheet pan with aluminum foil.

2. Place the lemon slices on the prepared sheet pan. Lay the salmon fillets, skin-side down, on the lemon slices.

3. In a small bowl, whisk the melted ghee, lemon juice, maple syrup, and garlic to combine. Spoon three-quarters of the ghee mixture over the salmon and reserve the rest. Season the salmon fillets with salt, pepper, and paprika.

4. Place another piece of foil over the salmon and seal the packet by folding the edges together.

5. Bake for 18 minutes. Remove the top piece of foil and drizzle the salmon with the remaining ghee mixture.

6. Turn the oven to broil.

7. Place the salmon under the broiler and cook for 5 minutes, or until golden. Serve garnished with chives (if using).

Substitution Tip: Select firm, white, wild-caught fish (see page 3) for this recipe.

Per Serving

Macronutrients: 57% Fat, 34% Protein, 9% Carbs

Calories: 409; Total Fat: 26g; Saturated Fat: 14g; Protein: 35g; Total Carbs: 8g; Fiber: 2g; Net Carbs: 6g; Cholesterol: 168mg

Sheet Pan Cod and Tricolor Peppers

DAIRY-FREE, EGG-FREE, NUT-FREE

Cod is a firm, white, flaky fish that is a good source of protein, niacin, and vitamin B$_{12}$. It holds up well to roasting. You will know your fish is cooked through when it flakes easily with a fork and turns opaque.

Serves 4   Prep time: 15 minutes / Cook time: 21 minutes

1½ pounds cod fillets
½ teaspoon salt, plus more as needed
½ teaspoon garlic powder
¼ teaspoon freshly ground black pepper, plus more as needed
1 large red bell pepper, sliced
1 large green bell pepper, sliced
1 large yellow bell pepper, sliced
4 tablespoons extra-virgin olive oil, divided
1 teaspoon Italian seasoning
¼ cup sliced green olives
Juice of 1 lemon
Lemon wedges, for serving (optional)

1. Preheat the oven to 400°F. Season the fish with salt, garlic powder, and pepper. Set aside.

2. Spread the red, green, and yellow bell peppers on a sheet pan and drizzle with 2 tablespoons of olive oil and the Italian seasoning. Toss to coat. Season with salt and pepper.

3. Roast the peppers for 15 minutes, or until they soften and start to caramelize around the edges.

4. Increase the oven temperature to 500°F. Push the peppers to the edges of the sheet pan. Place the fish fillets in the middle and sprinkle with the olives. Drizzle with the remaining 2 tablespoons of olive oil.

5. Roast for 6 minutes, or until the fish turns opaque and is cooked through.

6. Drizzle with lemon juice and season with salt and pepper. Serve with lemon wedges (if using).

Substitution Tip: Black olives can be substituted for green olives, or use a combination.

Per Serving

Macronutrients: 42% Fat, 45% Protein, 13% Carbs

Calories: 345; Total Fat: 16g; Saturated Fat: 2g; Protein: 39g; Total Carbs: 10g; Fiber: 3g; Net Carbs: 7g; Cholesterol: 94mg

Sheet Pan Fish and Chips

EGG-FREE

If you thought that fish and chips were out of the picture, I'm pleased to tell you this is not the case! Radishes stand in for the "chips" in this recipe, and are delicious when roasted. So much so, you won't miss the potato chips from your past.

Serves 4 **Prep time: 10 minutes / Cook time: 10 minutes**

¼ cup almond flour
½ teaspoon Old Bay seasoning
½ teaspoon salt
½ teaspoon freshly ground black pepper
1 pound cod fillets
4 tablespoons melted ghee, divided
1 pound large radishes, halved
1 lemon, quartered

1. Preheat the oven to 400°F. Line a large sheet pan with parchment paper.
2. In a small bowl, stir together the almond flour, Old Bay, salt, and pepper.
3. Place the cod on the prepared sheet pan and evenly distribute the almond flour mixture on each piece of fish.
4. Drizzle 2 tablespoons of ghee over the fish.
5. Place the radishes around the fish.
6. Drizzle the remaining 2 tablespoons of ghee over the radishes. Season the radishes with salt and pepper.
7. Bake for 10 minutes, or until the fish easily flakes with a fork and the radishes are hot. Serve with lemon wedges for squeezing.

Ingredient Tip: Frying the cod is also an option, although it will no longer be a one-pot meal. Stir together the almond flour and Old Bay and dip the fish in an egg wash, then dip in the almond flour mixture. Fry the fish in a skillet with oil.

Per Serving

Macronutrients: 57% Fat, 32% Protein, 11% Carbs

Calories: 284; Total Fat: 18g; Saturated Fat: 9g; Protein: 23g; Total Carbs: 8g; Fiber: 4g; Net Carbs: 4g; Cholesterol: 70mg

Shrimp and Sausage with Asparagus

DAIRY-FREE, EGG-FREE, NUT-FREE

Precooked sausage links can be a tricky ingredient because there may be ingredients in them that are not Paleo, so be sure to look for a Paleo-friendly sausage. The sausages should have an animal casing such as from pork, lamb, or beef. The filler should be only meat, fat, salt, and spices and possibly a sweetener, such as maple syrup.

Serves 4   **Prep time: 15 minutes / Cook time: 20 minutes**

1 pound precooked
  chicken sausage
  links, sliced
1 pound asparagus
  stalks, woody
  ends removed
1 large onion, sliced
1 tablespoon extra-virgin
  olive oil, divided
1 teaspoon salt, divided
1 pound raw shrimp,
  peeled and deveined
1 teaspoon Old Bay
  seasoning
Freshly ground
  black pepper
Juice of 1 lemon

1. Preheat the oven to 400°F.

2. Arrange the sausage, asparagus, and onion on a sheet pan. Drizzle with 1½ teaspoons of olive oil and ½ teaspoon of salt.

3. Roast for 10 minutes.

4. Remove the pan from the oven and add the shrimp. Season everything with the remaining ½ teaspoon of salt, Old Bay, and pepper. Drizzle with lemon juice.

5. Roast for 7 minutes more, or until the sausage is warmed through and the shrimp are pink.

Cooking Tip: Arrange the ingredients, starting on the diagonal of the sheet pan, in rows. Start with the onion, then place the asparagus next to the onion, the sausage next to the asparagus, and then the shrimp. If desired, cut another lemon into slices and arrange the lemon on the pan when the shrimp are added.

Per Serving

Macronutrients: 36% Fat, 47% Protein, 17% Carbs

Calories: 324; Total Fat: 13g; Saturated Fat: 4g; Protein: 38g; Total Carbs: 12g; Fiber: 4g; Net Carbs: 8g; Cholesterol: 236mg

Garlic Shrimp with Asparagus

EGG-FREE, NUT-FREE

Garlic not only adds great flavor to your food but is also highly nutirtious. It's rich in vitamins B₆ and C and magnesium. It also pairs extremely well with seafood and butter.

Serves 6   Prep time: 15 minutes / Cook time: 15 minutes

3 tablespoons
  ghee, divided
2 scallions, white part
  only, sliced
6 garlic cloves, minced
1 teaspoon minced
  peeled fresh ginger
1 pound raw shrimp,
  peeled and deveined
1 teaspoon salt
½ teaspoon freshly
  ground black pepper
1½ pounds asparagus,
  woody ends removed,
  spears cut into
  bite-size pieces
1 cup halved cherry
  tomatoes
1 tablespoon freshly
  squeezed lemon juice
½ teaspoon red pepper
  flakes (optional)

1. In a large skillet over medium heat, heat 2 tablespoons of ghee. Add the scallions, garlic, and ginger. Cook, stirring, for 1 minute.

2. Add the shrimp to the skillet and season with salt and pepper. Sauté for 3 minutes.

3. Return the skillet to the heat and add the remaining 1 tablespoon of ghee and asparagus. Sauté for 4 minutes, or until crisp-tender.

4. Stir in the tomatoes and sauté for 1 minute more. Return the shrimp to the skillet and stir in the lemon juice. Cook for 1 minute.

5. Sprinkle with red pepper flakes (if using) before serving.

Substitution Tip: For a Mexican flavor profile. In step 3, season the shrimp with 1 tablespoon chili powder, 2 teaspoons cumin, and the salt and pepper.

Per Serving

Macronutrients: 42% Fat, 40% Protein, 18% Carbs

Calories: 170; Total Fat: 8g; Saturated Fat: 5g; Protein: 17g; Total Carbs: 9g; Fiber: 3g; Net Carbs: 6g; Cholesterol: 105mg

Italian Seafood Bowl

DAIRY-FREE, EGG-FREE, NUT-FREE

This trio of seafood in a large bowl of Italian-flavored sauce is a delicious heartwarming recipe to serve your family. It will make them feel like you're treating them to a night out at their favorite Italian restaurant—right at home! Because pasta is out of the picture in a Paleo diet, serve this over zucchini noodles or cauliflower rice.

Serves 4   **Prep time: 15 minutes / Cook time: 25 minutes**

2 tablespoons
extra-virgin olive oil

½ cup chopped onion

4 garlic cloves, minced

2 cups chicken
broth, divided

8 ounces raw shrimp,
peeled and deveined

8 ounces scallops

8 ounces cod or haddock,
roughly cut

¾ cup tomato sauce

2 tablespoons
tomato paste

2 teaspoons minced
fresh oregano

2 teaspoons minced
fresh basil

½ teaspoon salt

¼ teaspoon freshly
ground black pepper

1. In a large stockpot over medium heat, heat the olive oil.

2. Add the onion and garlic and cook for 2 minutes, or until the onion is translucent.

3. Add ½ cup of chicken broth to the pot and simmer for 3 minutes, or until the broth evaporates by half.

4. Add the shrimp, scallops, and cod. Cook for 4 minutes, or until the cod starts to flake.

5. Stir in the tomato sauce, tomato paste, and remaining 1½ cups of chicken broth.

6. Stir in the oregano, basil, salt, and pepper. Bring the mixture to a boil, then reduce the heat to maintain a simmer. Cook for 15 minutes until the flavors meld.

Ingredient Tip: Buy all the seafood for this recipe on the same day you plan to make it. That way you will have the freshest seafood available for the best-tasting meal.

Per Serving

Macronutrients: 30% Fat, 52% Protein, 18% Carbs

Calories: 244; Total Fat: 8g; Saturated Fat: 2g; Protein: 32g; Total Carbs: 10g; Fiber: 2g; Net Carbs: 8g; Cholesterol: 109mg

Shrimp, Sweet Potato, and Arugula Bowl

EGG-FREE, NUT-FREE

Arugula is a nutrient-dense herb and a great source of calcium and fiber, making it a nutritious addition to this dish. As dairy is not consumed in a Paleo diet, getting extra calcium is a bonus. Combining the shrimp, sweet potato, and arugula brings together a blend of nutritional benefits that can help promote bone, heart, and brain health.

Serves 6   Prep time: 15 minutes / Cook time: 25 minutes

2 tablespoons ghee

½ cup chopped onion

3 garlic cloves, minced

1 large sweet
   potato, chopped

1½ pounds raw shrimp,
   peeled and deveined

4 cups arugula

Juice of 1 lemon

¾ teaspoon salt

½ teaspoon freshly
   ground black pepper

1. In a large skillet over medium heat, melt the ghee. Add the onion and garlic and cook for 2 minutes, or until the onion is softened.

2. Add the sweet potato and toss to coat. Cook for 15 minutes, stirring occasionally, until the sweet potato is easily pierced with a fork and slightly browned.

3. Add the shrimp and cook for 4 minutes, or until they are pink and have turned opaque.

4. Remove the skillet from the heat and add the arugula, tossing to wilt.

5. Season with lemon juice, salt, and pepper.

Substitution Tip: Reduce the carbs: Substitute 2 cups chopped zucchini for the sweet potato. It will still be delicious but only have 5 net carbs.

Per Serving

Macronutrients: 25% Fat, 48% Protein, 27% Carbs

Calories: 183; Total Fat: 5g; Saturated Fat: 3g; Protein: 22g; Total Carbs: 10g; Fiber: 2g; Net Carbs: 8g; Cholesterol: 145mg

Jalapeño Shrimp and "Grits"

EGG-FREE

To get that "grits" feel in this recipe, I use cauliflower, but it needs to be processed in smaller pieces than cauliflower rice, almost a purée, but not quite. I recommend buying a head of cauliflower and preparing it ahead of time by processing in a food processor and refrigerating until needed.

Serves 6   Prep time: 15 minutes / Cook time: 25 minutes

2 tablespoons
  ghee, divided
2 large garlic
  cloves, minced
1½ pounds raw shrimp,
  peeled and deveined
1 teaspoon Cajun
  seasoning
1½ teaspoons salt,
  divided, plus more
  as needed
1 jalapeño
  pepper, chopped
4 cups finely riced
  cauliflower
½ teaspoon freshly
  ground black pepper,
  plus more as needed
½ cup coconut cream
2 tablespoons nutritional
  yeast flakes
1½ teaspoons honey
  (optional)
½ teaspoon sriracha
  (optional)

1. In a large skillet over medium heat, melt 1 table-spoon of ghee. Add the garlic and sauté for 30 seconds, or until fragrant but not browned.

2. Add the shrimp to the skillet and season with the Cajun seasoning and ½ teaspoon of salt. Cook for 3 minutes, stirring often, until the shrimp are opaque. Remove the shrimp from the skillet and set aside. Wipe the skillet clean with a paper towel,

3. Return the skillet to the heat and add the remaining 1 tablespoon of ghee to melt.

4. Stir in the jalapeño and cook for 1 minute.

5. Add the cauliflower and season with the remaining 1 teaspoon of salt and the pepper. Cook for 10 min-utes, stirring occasionally.

6. Stir in the coconut cream and nutritional yeast flakes. Simmer for 10 minutes, or until the mixture is soft and smooth and looks like grits. Remove from the heat. Taste and season with salt and pepper, as needed.

7. Arrange the cooked shrimp over the cauliflower grits.

8. In a small bowl, stir together the honey (if using) and sriracha (if using). Place strategic dots of the honey sauce in a decorative pattern over the cauliflower grits.

Cooking Tip: In step 5, after the cauliflower has been added, if you don't hear it start to sizzle soon, turn up the heat a bit. This is the point when the water should begin to cook out of the cauliflower. The water should almost be evaporated by the time you stir in the coconut milk in step 6.

Per Serving

Macronutrients: 39% Fat, 47% Protein, 14% Carbs

Calories: 206; Total Fat: 9g; Saturated Fat: 6g; Protein: 24g; Total Carbs: 5g; Fiber: 2g; Net Carbs: 3g; Cholesterol: 145mg

Coconut Curry Shrimp and Zoodles

DAIRY-FREE, EGG-FREE

The coconut sauce for this recipe is made in the same skillet as the shrimp. There is no need to wipe out the skillet after the shrimp has been cooked, as the flavorful bits in the pan from cooking the shrimp add flavor to the coconut sauce. Serve with raw or lightly steamed zucchini noodles, if desired.

Serves 6   Prep time: 15 minutes / Cook time: 15 minutes

For the shrimp

1 tablespoon coconut oil

1 pound raw shrimp, peeled and deveined

1 teaspoon ground cumin

½ teaspoon chili powder

Salt

Freshly ground black pepper

For the sauce

1 cup full-fat coconut milk

½ cup chicken broth

½ cup almond butter

2 tablespoons coconut aminos

⅓ teaspoon salt

½ teaspoon red pepper flakes

½ teaspoon fish sauce

½ teaspoon grated peeled fresh ginger

2 zucchini, spiralized

To make the shrimp

1. In a large skillet over medium heat, heat the coconut oil until hot.

2. Add the shrimp, cumin, and chili powder. Season with salt and pepper. Toss to coat the shrimp with the seasonings.

3. Cook for 4 minutes, or until the shrimp have turned pink and are opaque. Remove from the skillet and set aside.

To make the sauce

1. Return the skillet to the heat and add the coconut milk, chicken broth, and almond butter. Whisk to combine.

2. Stir in the coconut aminos, salt, red pepper flakes, fish sauce, and ginger. Bring the sauce to a boil. Reduce the heat to maintain a simmer and cook for 7 minutes, or until the mixture begins to thicken.

3. Return the shrimp to the skillet and stir to coat the shrimp with the sauce. Serve over the zoodles.

Ingredient Tip: I love to serve zucchini noodles raw. However, it is very easy to give them a quick steam in the same skillet you cook the shrimp and sauce in. Before you cook the shrimp, place the noodles in a large skillet with a small amount of water and cover with an airtight lid. Once the skillet starts to steam, simmer the noodles for 1 minute. Remove from the skillet and set aside while you finish the recipe.

Per Serving
Macronutrients: 63% Fat, 25% Protein, 12% Carbs
Calories: 302; Total Fat: 21g; Saturated Fat: 9g; Protein: 19g; Total Carbs: 10g; Fiber: 3g; Net Carbs: 7g; Cholesterol: 90mg

Shrimp and Butternut Squash in Coconut Milk

DAIRY-FREE, EGG-FREE

Jalapeños are rich in vitamins A and C as well as potassium. Depending on the individual pepper, they can range from mild to hot. I love to add a little spicy heat to a recipe that has a natural sweetness. The sweet squash and coconut milk add to that contrast with the jalapeño in this recipe.

Serves 4   **Prep time: 15 minutes / Cook time: 20 minutes**

1 (13.5-ounce) can full-fat coconut milk

¾ cup chicken broth

2 teaspoons tomato paste

1½ teaspoons honey

1 teaspoon salt

¼ teaspoon red pepper flakes

¼ teaspoon freshly ground black pepper

2 cups chopped peeled butternut squash

1 cup julienned red bell pepper

1 jalapeño pepper, julienned (optional)

1 pound raw shrimp, peeled and deveined

2 cups cooked cauliflower rice

¼ cup freshly squeezed lime juice

¼ cup minced fresh cilantro

1. In a large Dutch oven over medium-high heat, whisk the coconut milk, chicken broth, tomato paste, honey, salt, red pepper flakes, and black pepper to combine.

2. Stir in the butternut squash, red bell pepper, and jalapeño (if using). Bring the mixture to a boil. Reduce the heat to maintain a simmer and cook for 10 minutes, or until the squash is easily pierced with a fork.

3. Stir in the shrimp and return the mixture to a boil.

4. Add the cauliflower rice, lime juice, and cilantro. Cook for 2 minutes, or until the cauliflower is tender.

Leftovers Tip: When you make Cauliflower Fried Rice (page 74), make extra and keep it refrigerated during the week. You only need to take the cauliflower out of the refrigerator and add it to the pot!

Per Serving

Macronutrients: 46% Fat, 28% Protein, 26% Carbs

Calories: 355; Total Fat: 18g; Saturated Fat: 15g; Protein: 25g; Total Carbs: 23g; Fiber: 5g; Net Carbs: 18g; Cholesterol: 136mg

Easy Cod Curry

DAIRY-FREE, EGG-FREE

Cod is my husband's favorite fish. Because of this, I love to find a variety of ways to prepare it. It has a mild flavor and firm texture that stand up well to recipes with strong spices such as this curry. It is also packed with protein, B vitamins, and minerals.

Serves 4   **Prep time: 10 minutes / Cook time: 20 minutes**

1½ teaspoons
  coconut oil
1 small onion, chopped
2 garlic cloves, minced
1 teaspoon minced
  peeled fresh ginger
2 teaspoons yellow
  curry powder
1 (13.5-ounce) can full-fat
  coconut milk
1 tablespoon freshly
  squeezed lime juice
Salt
Freshly ground
  black pepper
1 pound cod fillet, cut
  into 4 pieces
Chopped fresh cilantro,
  for garnish (optional)
Lime wedges, for serving
  (optional)

1. In a large nonstick skillet over medium-high heat, melt the coconut oil. Stir in the onion and sauté for 2 minutes, or until translucent.

2. Stir in the garlic, ginger, and curry powder. Fry for 1 minute, stirring occasionally.

3. Whisk in the coconut milk and lime juice. Season with salt and pepper. Bring the mixture to a boil, then reduce the heat to maintain a simmer.

4. Add the fish to the sauce and simmer for 10 minutes, or until the fish flakes easily with a fork.

5. Serve garnished with cilantro (if using) and with lime wedges (if using) for squeezing.

Leftovers Tip: Most curries are served with a side of rice. This is where precooked cauliflower rice comes in handy. I like to keep at least 4 cups of precooked cauliflower rice (plain with no seasoning) in the refrigerator for the week. Just reheat and eat.

Per Serving

Macronutrients: 56% Fat, 33% Protein, 11% Carbs

Calories: 324; Total Fat: 20g; Saturated Fat: 17g; Protein: 27g; Total Carbs: 5g; Fiber: 1g; Net Carbs: 4g; Cholesterol: 62mg

Sesame Chicken, page 122

Chapter Six

POULTRY

Asian-Style Turkey Lettuce Cups

DAIRY-FREE, EGG-FREE

You may read the words "rice vinegar" and think: not Paleo approved. Rice vinegar is fermented rice and although the cave dwellers probably weren't fermenting their food, it is allowed on this diet. Fermented foods have health benefits of their own. Vinegar can help improve insulin sensitivity and lower blood sugar.

Serves 4   Prep time: 10 minutes / Cook time: 20 minutes

1 tablespoon coconut oil

1 pound ground turkey

²/₃ cup chopped red bell pepper

3 tablespoons coconut aminos

2 tablespoons unseasoned rice vinegar

2 tablespoons honey

1 teaspoon chili paste

1 teaspoon sesame oil

8 Butter lettuce leaves

1. In a large skillet over medium heat, melt the coconut oil. Add the ground turkey and cook for 10 minutes, stirring to break up the meat, or until the turkey is no longer pink.

2. Add the red bell pepper and cook for 5 minutes until the pepper begins to soften.

3. Stir in the coconut aminos, vinegar, honey, chili paste, and sesame oil. Toss until well combined. Cook for 1 minute.

4. Arrange the lettuce cups on a serving plate and evenly divide the turkey mixture between them.

Ingredient Tip: Sesame oil should be used in moderation in a Paleo diet. In this recipe, it is added for flavor after the cooking is done.

Per Serving

Macronutrients: 49% Fat, 35% Protein, 16% Carbs

Calories: 365; Total Fat: 20g; Saturated Fat: 7g; Protein: 32g; Total Carbs: 14g; Fiber: 1g; Net Carbs: 13g; Cholesterol: 116mg

Chicken Cabbage Stir-Fry

EGG-FREE, NUT-FREE

I like to use smoked paprika in this stir-fry because I love the color and earthy flavor the spice lends. Smoked paprika is made from dried red peppers of the Capsicum annuum *variety (think: bell pepper) that are smoked over an oak fire, then finely ground into a powder.*

Serves 4   Prep time: 10 minutes / Cook time: 27 minutes

2 tablespoons ghee, divided

1 pound chicken breasts, cut into bite-size pieces

1 teaspoon salt

½ teaspoon freshly ground black pepper

½ cup chopped onion

1 carrot, shredded

1 head green cabbage, chopped

2 garlic cloves, minced

1 teaspoon smoked paprika

1. In a large skillet over medium heat, melt 1 tablespoon of ghee until hot.

2. Add the chicken to the skillet and season with salt and pepper. Sauté for 7 minutes, or until the chicken is no longer pink. Remove the chicken from the skillet and set aside.

3. Return the skillet to the heat and add the remaining 1 tablespoon of ghee, the onion, and the carrot. Sauté for 3 minutes, or until the carrot begins to soften.

4. Add the cabbage and cook for 15 minutes, stirring often, or until the cabbage softens.

5. Stir in the garlic and paprika.

6. Return the chicken to the skillet and toss with the cabbage mixture. Cook for 2 minutes to warm.

Substitution Tip: Skip steps 1 and 2 and substitute 2 cups chopped rotisserie chicken for the chicken breast in this recipe. Stir the chicken in at step 6 and cook until heated through.

Per Serving

Macronutrients: 36% Fat, 43% Protein, 11% Carbs

Calories: 250; Total Fat: 10g; Saturated Fat: 5g; Protein: 27g; Total Carbs: 17g; Fiber: 6g; Net Carbs: 11g; Cholesterol: 80mg

Skillet Chicken and Peppers

EGG-FREE, NUT-FREE

Bell peppers are an excellent vegetable to consume on the Paleo diet. They are rich in vitamins A and C and potassium as well as high in fiber. They may help improve eye health and reduce the risk of chronic diseases. They are low in carbs and delicious when sautéed.

Serves 4   Prep time: 15 minutes / Cook time: 20 minutes

1 tablespoon ghee
1 pound boneless, skinless chicken breasts, cut into thin strips
½ cup sliced onion
½ cup chopped green bell pepper
½ cup chopped red bell pepper
1 jalapeño pepper, seeded and chopped
¾ cup water
½ cup tomato sauce
1½ teaspoons chili powder
½ teaspoon ground cumin
1 teaspoon salt

1. In a large skillet over medium heat, melt the ghee.

2. Add the chicken and cook for 7 minutes, or until no longer pink.

3. Stir in the onion, green and red bell peppers, and jalapeño. Cook, stirring frequently, for 4 minutes, or until the peppers soften.

4. Stir in ¾ cup water with the tomato sauce, chili powder, cumin, and salt. Bring the chicken mixture to a boil, then reduce the heat to maintain a simmer. Cook for 5 minutes, or until the sauce has slightly thickened.

Substitution Tip: Add a little splash of color to this recipe by substituting yellow bell pepper for the red bell pepper.

Per Serving

Macronutrients: 31% Fat, 55% Protein, 14% Carbs

Calories: 175; Total Fat: 6g; Saturated Fat: 3g; Protein: 24g; Total Carbs: 7g; Fiber: 2g; Net Carbs: 5g; Cholesterol: 73mg

Turkey and Brussels Sprouts Stir-Fry

EGG-FREE

Brussels sprouts are high in fiber and are a nutritious addition to your diet. They may help reduce the risk of cancer, decrease inflammation, and improve blood sugar. The caramelization of the Brussels sprouts adds incredible flavor to this recipe.

Serves 4   **Prep time: 15 minutes / Cook time: 20 minutes**

4 tablespoons
  ghee, divided
1½ teaspoons minced
  peeled fresh ginger
2 garlic cloves, minced
1 pound ground
  turkey breast
1 pound Brussels
  sprouts, halved
  lengthwise
2 tablespoons
  coconut aminos
½ teaspoon salt
¼ teaspoon freshly
  ground black pepper
Chopped fresh cilantro,
  for garnish (optional)

1. In a large skillet over medium heat, melt 2 tablespoons of ghee. Add the ginger and garlic. Sauté for 2 minutes.

2. Add the ground turkey and cook for 7 minutes, stirring to break up the meat, or until no longer pink. Remove the turkey from the skillet and set aside.

3. Return the skillet to the heat and add the remaining 2 tablespoons of ghee to melt.

4. Stir in the Brussels sprouts. Stir-fry for 5 minutes until they begin to brown and become tender.

5. Return the turkey to the skillet and stir in the coconut aminos, salt, and pepper. Cook for 2 minutes, or until hot.

6. Serve garnished with cilantro (if using).

   Substitution Tip: If you cannot find fresh Brussels sprouts, use frozen. Broccoli or cauliflower can also be used in place of the Brussels sprouts.

Per Serving

Macronutrients: 44% Fat, 41% Protein, 15% Carbs

Calories: 304; Total Fat: 15g; Saturated Fat: 8g;
Protein: 31g; Total Carbs: 12g; Fiber: 4g; Net Carbs: 8g;
Cholesterol: 94mg

Sheet Pan Chicken and Asparagus

DAIRY-FREE, EGG-FREE

Roasting your dinner on a sheet pan is one of the best ways to extract flavor from food. The roasted vegetables have a caramelized layer that makes the recipe feel rustic, hearty, and warm.

Serves 4   Prep time: 10 minutes / Cook time: 30 minutes

4 (4-ounce) skin-on chicken breasts
1 teaspoon salt
½ teaspoon freshly ground black pepper
⅓ cup freshly squeezed lemon juice
2 tablespoons honey
1 tablespoon coconut aminos
2 garlic cloves, minced
1 pound asparagus, woody ends removed
Lemon wedges, for serving (optional)

1. Preheat the oven to 400°F. Line a sheet pan with parchment paper.

2. Arrange the chicken on the prepared sheet pan and season with salt and pepper.

3. In a small bowl, whisk the lemon juice, honey, coconut aminos, and garlic to blend. Brush the mixture over the chicken breast.

4. Bake for 20 minutes, or until the internal temperature of the chicken reaches 165°F, or until the juices run clear.

5. Remove the pan from the oven and arrange the asparagus around the cooked chicken.

6. Bake for 7 minutes more, or until the asparagus is cooked.

7. Serve with lemon wedges for squeezing (if using).

Option Tip: Marinate the chicken overnight in the lemon juice marinade. When the chicken is placed on the parchment paper, season it with salt and pepper and proceed to step 4.

Per Serving

Macronutrients: 27% Fat, 49% Protein, 24% Carbs

Calories: 263; Total Fat: 8g; Saturated Fat: 2g; Protein: 32g; Total Carbs: 15g; Fiber: 2g; Net Carbs: 13g; Cholesterol: 82mg

Chicken Tenders with Mushrooms and Pearl Onions

EGG-FREE, NUT-FREE

Arrowroot powder is a common substitute for cornstarch and is completely Paleo friendly. It is very versatile and can be used to coat meat and vegetables as well as to thicken sauces.

Serves 4   **Prep time: 10 minutes / Cook time: 20 minutes**

2 tablespoons ghee, divided

1 pound chicken tenderloins

1 teaspoon salt

½ teaspoon freshly ground black pepper

1 (14.4-ounce) package frozen pearl onions

8 ounces baby portobello mushrooms, quartered

1⅔ cups chicken broth, divided

2 teaspoons arrowroot powder

1 teaspoon chopped fresh thyme

1. In a large skillet over medium heat, melt 1 tablespoon of ghee.

2. Add the chicken tenders, season with salt and pepper, and sauté for 4 minutes, or until opaque. Remove the chicken from the skillet and set aside.

3. Return the skillet to the heat and add the remaining 1 tablespoon of ghee to melt. Stir in the onions and mushrooms and cook for 3 minutes, stirring occasionally.

4. Stir ⅔ cup of chicken broth into the skillet to deglaze it, scraping up any browned bits from the bottom. Simmer for 3 minutes until reduced.

5. In a small bowl, whisk the remaining 1 cup of chicken broth and arrowroot powder. Add the slurry to the skillet and bring to a boil. Reduce the heat and cook until thickened, 2 to 3 minutes.

6. Return the chicken tenders to the skillet and bring the mixture to a boil. Remove from the heat and garnish with thyme.

Substitution Tip: Substitute a dry white wine for the ⅔ cup chicken broth used to deglaze the skillet in step 4.

Per Serving

Macronutrients: 35% Fat, 48% Protein, 17% Carbs

Calories: 207; Total Fat: 8g; Saturated Fat: 5g; Protein: 25g; Total Carbs: 8g; Fiber: 1g; Net Carbs: 7g; Cholesterol: 87mg

Turkey Tenderloins with Creamy Basil Tomato Sauce

EGG-FREE

Turkey tenderloins are a perfect match for the creamy basil tomato sauce in this recipe. However, they may be more difficult to find in the store and can sometimes be costly. Don't let this stop you from trying the recipe; you can substitute chicken tenderloins for the turkey.

Serves 6   **Prep time: 10 minutes / Cook time: 25 minutes**

1½ tablespoons ghee
½ onion, chopped
3 garlic cloves, minced
1 pound turkey
　tenderloins
1 cup chicken broth
1 cup coconut cream
½ cup tomato sauce
¼ teaspoon dried thyme
¼ teaspoon
　dried oregano
¼ teaspoon dried basil
¼ teaspoon red
　pepper flakes
¼ cup cold water
½ teaspoon
　arrowroot powder
Chopped fresh basil, for
　garnish (optional)

1. In a large skillet over medium heat, melt the ghee.
2. Add the onion and garlic and sauté for 3 minutes, or until the onion is translucent.
3. Add the turkey tenderloins and cook for 5 minutes, or until lightly browned.
4. Add the chicken broth to the skillet and bring to a boil. Reduce the heat to maintain a simmer and stir in the coconut cream, tomato sauce, thyme, oregano, basil, and red pepper flakes. Simmer for 10 minutes.
5. In a small bowl, whisk ¼ cup cold water and the arrowroot powder to combine. Stir the slurry into the skillet and cook for 2 minutes until the sauce begins to thicken.
6. Serve garnished with basil (if using).

Ingredient Tip: If the sauce, as is, is thick enough for you, eliminate the arrowroot powder slurry.

Per Serving

Macronutrients: 52% Fat, 39% Protein, 9% Carbs

Calories: 207; Total Fat: 12g; Saturated Fat: 9g; Protein: 20g; Total Carbs: 3g; Fiber: 1g; Net Carbs: 2g; Cholesterol: 55mg

Turkey Bolognese Sauce

DAIRY-FREE, EGG-FREE, NUT-FREE

Turkey is rich in niacin and other B vitamins, and contains anticancer properties as well as tryptophan. This sauce is as simple as putting all the ingredients into the slow cooker, giving it a stir, then forgetting about it for the next 6 hours. Shape the ground turkey into 1-inch meatballs, if you desire.

Serves 6 **Prep time: 5 minutes / Cook time: 6 hours**

1 pound ground turkey

1 (28-ounce) can tomato sauce

1 (6-ounce) can tomato paste

½ cup chicken broth

2 garlic cloves, minced

2 teaspoons Italian seasoning

1 teaspoon salt

½ teaspoon freshly ground black pepper

1. Crumble the ground turkey into the bottom of the slow cooker.

2. Stir in the tomato sauce, tomato paste, chicken broth, garlic, Italian seasoning, salt, and pepper.

3. Cover the cooker and cook on low heat for 6 hours. Stir and serve.

Option Tip: If you wish to serve this with zucchini noodles, place the sauce on top of the noodles (raw), or stir 2 cups of zucchini noodles into the finished sauce. The heat from the sauce will soften the noodles.

Instant Pot Tip: Select Sauté and add 1 tablespoon extra-virgin olive oil to heat. Add the ground turkey and cook, breaking it up in pieces, until it begins to brown. Turn off the Instant Pot. Stir in the chicken broth to deglaze the bottom of the pot. Stir in the remaining ingredients. Lock the lid in place and seal the vent. Select Manual and cook on High for 5 minutes. Quick release the pressure to finish.

Per Serving

Macronutrients: 48% Fat, 34% Protein, 18% Carbs

Calories: 260; Total Fat: 14g; Saturated Fat: 4g; Protein: 22g; Total Carbs: 15g; Fiber: 4g; Net Carbs: 11g; Cholesterol: 81 mg

Chicken Thighs with Sun-Dried Tomato Cream

EGG-FREE

Sun-dried tomatoes have an intense flavor. They are a concentrated source of nutrients, including vitamins C and K, iron, and lycopene, which is an antioxidant associated with a lower risk of certain cancers.

Serves 4   **Prep time: 10 minutes / Cook time: 25 minutes**

2 tablespoons ghee

1 pound boneless, skinless chicken thighs

1 cup chicken broth

½ cup dry-packed sun-dried tomatoes, julienned

½ cup coconut cream

4 garlic cloves, minced

2 teaspoons Italian seasoning

1 tablespoon nutritional yeast flakes (optional)

Chopped fresh basil, for garnish (optional)

1. In a large skillet over medium heat, melt the ghee.

2. Add the chicken and cook for 7 minutes per side, or until the chicken is browned and cooked through. Transfer the chicken to a plate and keep warm.

3. In the skillet, combine the chicken broth, sun-dried tomatoes, coconut cream, garlic, Italian seasoning, and nutritional yeast flakes (if using). Whisk to blend. Bring the sauce to a boil, then reduce the heat to maintain a simmer. Cook, uncovered, for 7 minutes until sauce begins to reduce and thicken.

4. Return the chicken to the skillet and spoon the sauce over it. Simmer for 5 minutes.

5. Serve garnished with basil (if using).

Ingredient Tip: If you can't find the dry packaged tomatoes, substitute the oil-packed, but be sure to drain the tomatoes first.

Per Serving

Macronutrients: 63% Fat, 28% Protein, 9% Carbs

Calories: 314; Total Fat: 22g; Saturated Fat: 12g; Protein: 22g; Total Carbs: 6g; Fiber: 1g; Net Carbs: 5g; Cholesterol: 129mg

Turkey-Stuffed Portobello Mushrooms

EGG-FREE, NUT-FREE

Portobello mushrooms are low in sodium, fat, and cholesterol. They are also a good source of protein and fiber. Sautéing the mushrooms in the ghee adds a rich, delicious meaty flavor and texture.

Serves 4 **Prep time: 10 minutes / Cook time: 20 minutes**

1 tablespoon ghee

4 large portobello mushroom caps

2 garlic cloves, minced

8 ounces ground turkey

2 cups fresh baby spinach leaves

½ cup halved grape tomatoes

½ teaspoon salt

¼ teaspoon freshly ground black pepper

1. In a large skillet over medium heat, melt the ghee. Place the mushrooms into the skillet and cook for 5 minutes per side, or until softened. Remove the mushrooms from the skillet and set aside on a plate.

2. In the same skillet, sauté the garlic for 1 minute.

3. Add the ground turkey and break it up into smaller pieces. Cook for 7 minutes, or until browned and no longer pink.

4. Stir in the spinach and grape tomatoes and cook for 2 minutes. Season with salt and pepper. Divide the turkey mixture evenly among the mushroom caps.

Option Tip: Instead of stirring in the tomatoes with the spinach in step 4, place them on top of the filled mushroom caps and broil for 2 to 3 minutes. This adds another level of flavor to the tomatoes. They will get hot and the skins will burst, giving the tomatoes a roasted flavor.

Per Serving

Macronutrients: 58% Fat, 36% Protein, 6% Carbs

Calories: 200; Total Fat: 13g; Saturated Fat: 5g; Protein: 18g; Total Carbs: 4g; Fiber: 1g; Net Carbs: 3g; Cholesterol: 68mg

Turkey Taco Stuffed Peppers

DAIRY-FREE, EGG-FREE, NUT-FREE

I use red peppers in this recipe because they pack the most nutrition of all the peppers, as they stay on the plant vine longer. They have more beta-carotene and 1½ times more vitamin C than their green and yellow counterparts. This recipe gives you a spicy taco flavor that complements the sweetness of the red pepper. You can use 1 cup frozen cauliflower rice in place of the fresh cauliflower rice and reduce the cook time in step 6 to 4 minutes.

Serves 4   Prep time: 15 minutes / Cook time: 1 hour, 5 minutes

1 tablespoon extra-virgin
  olive oil
½ small onion, chopped
2 garlic cloves, minced
1 pound ground turkey
2 tomatoes, chopped
1 cup cauliflower rice
2 tablespoons
  chili powder
1½ teaspoons
  ground cumin
1 teaspoon salt
½ teaspoon freshly
  ground black pepper
4 red bell
  peppers, halved
1 tablespoon chopped
  fresh cilantro (optional)

1. Preheat the oven to 350°F.

2. In a large oven-safe skillet over medium-high heat, heat the oil.

3. Add the onion and garlic and cook for 4 minutes, or until translucent.

4. Add the turkey and cook for 10 minutes, stirring to break up the meat, or until it is cooked through and no longer pink. Remove from the skillet and set aside.

5. Return the skillet to the heat and stir in the tomatoes, scraping up any browned bits from the bottom.

6. Stir in the cauliflower rice, chili powder, cumin, salt, and pepper. Cook for 8 minutes, stirring, or until the vegetables are soft.

7. Return the turkey to the skillet and simmer for 5 minutes. Remove from the heat and let cool for 10 minutes.

8. Fill each red pepper half with the turkey mixture and arrange the pepper halves in the skillet.

9. Bake, uncovered, for 25 minutes, or until the peppers are slightly softened.

10. Garnish with cilantro (if using).

Option Tip: Make these peppers with an Asian-style flair. Eliminate the chili powder and cumin and add 1 teaspoon sesame oil, 1 teaspoon ground ginger and 2 tablespoons coconut aminos. Top with the cilantro after baking.

Per Serving (2 pepper halves)

Macronutrients: 56% Fat, 32% Protein, 12% Carbs

Calories: 387; Total Fat: 24g; Saturated Fat: 6g; Protein: 31g; Total Carbs: 12g; Fiber: 4g; Net Carbs: 8g; Cholesterol: 120mg

Coconut Lime Chicken

EGG-FREE

I love lime. When it is mixed with coconut, I think it is a heavenly combination. Limes are a good source of magnesium and potassium. They help reduce inflammation and can help reduce heart disease. All the more reason to add a little lime to the coconut!

Serves 4 Prep time: 10 minutes / Cook time: 30 minutes

3 teaspoons ghee, divided
1½ pounds chicken breast tenders
½ teaspoon salt
¼ teaspoon freshly ground black pepper
½ small onion, chopped
1 jalapeño pepper, seeded and chopped
1 cup chicken broth
2 tablespoons freshly squeezed lime juice
½ cup coconut cream
Paprika, for seasoning (optional)
Chopped fresh cilantro, for garnish (optional)
Lime wedges, for serving (optional)

1. In a large skillet over medium-high heat, melt 1½ teaspoons of ghee.

2. Add the chicken breast tenders and season with the salt and pepper. Cook for 5 minutes per side, or until browned. Remove the chicken from the skillet and set aside. Wipe the skillet clean with a paper towel.

3. Return the skillet to the heat and add the remaining 1½ teaspoons of ghee to melt.

4. Stir in the onion and jalapeño and sauté for 2 minutes, or until soft.

5. Stir in the chicken broth and lime juice. Bring the mixture to a boil, then reduce the heat to maintain a simmer. Cook for 5 minutes.

6. Whisk in the coconut cream and bring to a simmer again. Cook for 5 minutes.

7. Add the chicken back to the skillet. Cover the skillet and cook for 10 minutes, or until the chicken is cooked all the way through.

8. Sprinkle with paprika (if using) and cilantro (if using). Serve with lime wedges (if using) for squeezing.

Cooking Tip: If you need to thicken the sauce, mix 1 teaspoon arrowroot powder with 1 tablespoon water and whisk the slurry into the hot sauce. Simmer for 1 minute before adding the chicken back to the pan.

Per Serving
Macronutrients: 37% Fat, 57% Protein, 6% Carbs
Calories: 267; Total Fat: 11g; Saturated Fat: 8g; Protein: 38g; Total Carbs: 1g; Fiber: 0g; Net Carbs: 1g; Cholesterol: 106mg

Sesame Chicken

DAIRY-FREE, EGG-FREE

This recipe is a Paleo take on one of our most favorite Chinese takeout dishes. This is my hubby's most requested! Even though this recipe uses a couple of bowls for prep, it is just too delicious not to share with you.

Serves 4   Prep time: 15 minutes / Cook time: 15 minutes

1 pound boneless, skinless chicken breasts, cut into thin strips

2 tablespoons arrowroot powder

½ teaspoon salt

¼ teaspoon freshly ground black pepper

3 tablespoons extra-virgin olive oil

½ cup chicken broth

¼ cup coconut aminos

1 tablespoon honey

2 teaspoons sesame oil

½ teaspoon fish sauce

¼ to ½ teaspoon red pepper flakes

2 tablespoons toasted sesame seeds (optional)

1 tablespoon chopped fresh chives (optional)

1. In a small bowl, toss together the chicken, arrowroot powder, salt, and pepper to coat.

2. Heat the olive oil in a large skillet over medium-high heat. Add the chicken, searing it on both sides, for 7 minutes total, until golden brown. To avoid overcrowding, cook the chicken in batches if needed.

3. In a small bowl, whisk together the chicken broth, coconut aminos, honey, sesame oil, fish sauce, and red pepper flakes. Pour the sauce into the skillet and deglaze the pan, stirring to scrape up any browned bits from the bottom.

4. Bring the sauce to a boil, then reduce the heat to maintain a simmer. Cook for 4 minutes, or until the sauce has thickened and reduced.

5. Garnish with sesame seeds (if using) and chives (if using).

Substitution Tip: This recipe also works well with shrimp. Substitute 1 pound shrimp for the chicken and proceed as directed.

Per Serving

Macronutrients: 50% Fat, 34% Protein, 16% Carbs

Calories: 268; Total Fat: 15g; Saturated Fat: 2g; Protein: 23g; Total Carbs: 11g; Fiber: 0g; Net Carbs: 11g; Cholesterol: 66mg

General Tso's Chicken

EGG-FREE

This is my favorite better-than-takeout recipe. I love the sweet-heat flavor combination, and this recipe brings it all to the table. The whole chile peppers in this recipe pack a lot of heat, so be sure to remove them from the dish when serving so no one bites into one by accident.

Serves 6   **Prep time: 15 minutes / Cook time: 15 minutes**

¼ cup water

3 tablespoons tomato paste

2 tablespoons honey

2 tablespoons coconut aminos

2 tablespoons rice vinegar

2 garlic cloves, minced

1 tablespoon ghee

1½ pounds chicken breasts, cut into bite-size pieces

½ teaspoon salt

¼ teaspoon freshly ground black pepper

1 tablespoon sesame oil

4 scallions, white and green parts, sliced, divided

1 teaspoon minced peeled fresh ginger

5 whole dried chile peppers

1. In a small bowl, whisk ¼ cup water, the tomato paste, honey, coconut aminos, vinegar, and garlic to combine. Set aside.

2. In a large skillet over medium-high heat, melt the ghee.

3. Add the chicken and season with salt and pepper. Cook for 7 minutes, stirring frequently, or until the chicken is browned on all sides and no longer pink. Remove the chicken from the skillet and set aside. Wipe the skillet clean with a paper towel.

4. Return the skillet to the heat and add the sesame oil, white scallion parts, and ginger. Sauté, stirring, for 1 minute.

5. Stir the sauce mixture into the skillet and add the chiles. Bring the mixture to a boil and cook for 2 minutes.

CONTINUED

General Tso's Chicken, CONTINUED

6. Add the chicken back to the sauce and toss to coat.

7. Garnish with the green scallion parts to serve.

Substitution Tip: Substitute ½ to 1 teaspoon red pepper flakes for the whole chiles. Depending on your heat sensitivity, add more or less.

Per Serving		
Macronutrients: 30% Fat, 46% Protein, 24% Carbs		
Calories: 208; Total Fat: 7g; Saturated Fat: 2g; Protein: 24g; Total Carbs: 12g; Fiber: 1g; Net Carbs: 11g; Cholesterol: 70mg		

Butter Chicken

EGG-FREE

The original Indian recipe for butter chicken is called so because the chicken is coated in a "butter" gravy that uses butter and cream. Because butter and cream are not allowed in a Paleo diet, I substitute ghee and coconut cream to make a similar but dairy-free gravy.

Serves 6 **Prep time: 15 minutes / Cook time: 6 hours, plus 20 minutes to simmer**

1 (13.5-ounce) can coconut cream

1 tablespoon ghee

1 small onion, chopped

4 garlic cloves, minced

1 (6-ounce) can tomato paste

1 tablespoon minced peeled fresh ginger

1 tablespoon yellow curry powder

2 teaspoons garam masala

1 teaspoon chili powder

1/2 teaspoon ground cumin

1 teaspoon salt

1/2 teaspoon freshly ground black pepper

2 pounds boneless, skinless chicken thighs, cut into bite-size pieces

1. Turn the slow cooker to high heat and let it warm up for 10 minutes.

2. In the heated slow cooker, combine the coconut cream and ghee and let melt. Whisk to blend.

3. Whisk in the onion, garlic, tomato paste, ginger, curry powder, garam masala, chili powder, cumin, salt, and pepper to combine.

4. Add the chicken and stir to coat.

5. Cover the cooker and reset the cooker to low heat. Cook for 6 hours.

6. Remove the cover from the slow cooker and adjust the heat to high. Simmer for 20 minutes, or until the sauce has reduced and thickened slightly.

CONTINUED

Butter Chicken, CONTINUED

Ingredient Tip: Garam masala is a blend of toasted spices used in Indian cooking. It is a warming spice with a sweetness that also lends a touch of heat from the pepper. Usually this blend consists of coriander, cumin, cardamom, cloves, cinnamon, and black pepper. There are several recipes on the internet for making this spice blend should you have a hard time finding it in the store.

Instant Pot Tip: Select the Sauté setting. Heat the coconut cream and ghee until warmed and whisk to combine. Add the ingredients in step 3 in the same order. Lock the lid in place and seal the vent. Select Manual and cook on High pressure for 10 minutes. Let the pressure release naturally for 10 minutes, then quick release the remaining pressure. Remove the lid and stir to combine before serving.

Per Serving

Macronutrients: 61% Fat, 29% Protein, 10% Carbs

Calories: 401; Total Fat: 27g; Saturated Fat: 15g; Protein: 29g; Total Carbs: 9g; Fiber: 3g; Net Carbs: 6g; Cholesterol: 155mg

Thai Chicken Curry

EGG-FREE

The ginger in this recipe is known to boost the immune system, relieve arthritis pain, improve heart health, and can help lower cholesterol. Ginger is also available pre-minced in jars or as a paste in the produce section and can be substituted for the fresh ginger in this recipe.

Serves 4   Prep time: 15 minutes / Cook time: 35 minutes

2 tablespoons ghee

1 pound boneless, skinless chicken thighs, cut into bite-size pieces

1 cup chopped peeled butternut squash

1 (13.5-ounce) can coconut cream

1 cup hot water

3 tablespoons red curry paste

1 tablespoon coconut aminos

1 tablespoon maple syrup

1 tablespoon minced peeled fresh ginger

2 teaspoons fish sauce

2 garlic cloves, minced

1. In a large skillet over medium heat, melt the ghee. Add the chicken and cook for 7 minutes, stirring frequently, until the chicken is lightly browned on all sides.

2. Stir in the butternut squash and cook for 5 minutes. Transfer the chicken and squash to a plate and set aside.

3. Return the skillet to the heat and whisk in the coconut cream, 1 cup hot water, the curry paste, coconut aminos, maple syrup, ginger, fish sauce, and garlic. Bring to a boil.

4. Return the chicken and squash to the skillet and stir to combine. Reduce the heat to maintain a simmer and cook for 20 minutes, or until the sauce has reduced and thickened and the squash is tender.

Substitution Tip: If you're out of red curry paste, substitute 2 teaspoons curry powder.

Per Serving
Macronutrients: 66% Fat, 19% Protein, 15% Carbs
Calories: 465; Total Fat: 34g; Saturated Fat: 22g; Protein: 22g; Total Carbs: 13g; Fiber: 2g; Net Carbs: 11g; Cholesterol: 128mg

Curried Turkey Meatballs

DAIRY-FREE, EGG-FREE

Although the ingredient list may seem long, it really isn't. The meatball ingredients and sauce ingredients include some of the same items, only used in a different way. You may spend all of your 15-minute prep time in this recipe, but it is well worth the result.

Serves 4 to 6   **Prep time: 15 minutes / Cook time: 40 minutes**

For the meatballs

1 pound ground turkey
**¼ cup chopped
  fresh basil**
2 garlic cloves, minced
2 tablespoons fish sauce
1 tablespoon honey
**1½ teaspoons red
  curry paste**
Salt
**Freshly ground
  black pepper**
**2 tablespoons
  extra-virgin olive
  oil, divided**

For the sauce

½ small onion, chopped
2 garlic cloves, minced
**1 (13.5-ounce) can
  coconut cream**
**1½ tablespoons red
  curry paste**
**1½ tablespoons freshly
  squeezed lime juice**
1½ teaspoons fish sauce
**Sliced fresh basil, for
  garnish (optional)**

To make the meatballs

1. In a large bowl, combine the turkey, basil, garlic, fish sauce, honey, and curry paste. Season with salt and pepper. Mix to combine. Shape the meat mixture into (about 24) 1-inch meatballs.

2. In a large skillet over medium heat, heat 1 tablespoon of olive oil. Place half the meatballs in the skillet and cook for 2 minutes per side until browned. Remove the meatballs from the skillet and set aside.

3. Return the skillet to the heat and add the remaining 1 tablespoon of olive oil to heat. Add the remaining meatballs and cook for 2 minutes per side until browned. Remove the meatballs and set aside. Drain all but 1 tablespoon of oil from the skillet.

To make the sauce

1. Return the skillet with the oil to the heat and add the onion. Sauté for 3 minutes, or until softened. Add the garlic and sauté for 2 minutes more until the garlic is lightly browned.

2. Whisk in the coconut cream and curry paste until smooth. Stir in the lime juice and fish sauce.Return the meatballs to the skillet and simmer in the sauce for 15 minutes.

3. Serve garnished with fresh basil (if using).

Cooking Tip: When browning the meatballs, do not crowd the skillet. Having the meatballs too close together does not let air circulate around the meatballs and they will be steamed rather than browned. This may mean frying them in batches.

Per Serving

Macronutrients: 68% Fat, 22% Protein, 10% Carbs

Calories: 439; Total Fat: 33g; Saturated Fat: 19g; Protein: 24g; Total Carbs: 8g; Fiber: 0g; Net Carbs: 8g; Cholesterol: 80mg

Pot Roast Dinner, page 156

Chapter Seven
BEEF AND PORK

Steak with Tomatoes and Green Beans

DAIRY-FREE, EGG-FREE, NUT-FREE

Sometimes just a simple cooked steak is the best meal ever. This recipe is seasoned just with salt and pepper and served with grape tomatoes and green beans sautéed in the same skillet. This meal is so satisfying you won't even miss the potatoes.

Serves 6   **Prep time: 10 minutes / Cook time: 15 minutes**

1½ pounds bone-in rib eye steak

1 teaspoon salt, divided

½ teaspoon freshly ground black pepper, divided

3 teaspoons extra-virgin olive oil, divided

2 bay leaves

1 pint grape tomatoes

2 cups trimmed green beans

Sprig of rosemary

1. Season the steak all over with ½ teaspoon of salt and ¼ teaspoon of pepper. Set aside.

2. In a large skillet over medium-high heat, warm 1½ teaspoons of olive oil. Add the bay leaves.

3. Add the steak and cook for 4 minutes per side for medium-rare. Adjust the cooking time as desired. Remove the steak from the skillet and set aside. Wipe the skillet clean with a paper towel.

4. Return the skillet to the heat and heat the remaining 1½ teaspoons of olive oil.

5. Add the tomatoes and green beans. Season with the remaining ½ teaspoon of salt and ¼ teaspoon of pepper. Cook, stirring occasionally, for 4 minutes until the green beans are crisp-tender, and serve alongside the steak. Top with rosemary sprig.

Substitution Tip: Substitute ghee for olive oil and add a few garlic cloves, crushed, and a thyme sprig to the skillet when adding the vegetables in step 5.

Per Serving

Macronutrients: 72% Fat, 24% Protein, 4% Carbs

Calories: 350; Total Fat: 28g; Saturated Fat: 11g; Protein: 21g; Total Carbs: 5g; Fiber: 2g; Net Carbs: 3g; Cholesterol: 76mg

Roasted Pork Loin with Vegetables

DAIRY-FREE, EGG-FREE, NUT-FREE

Shishito peppers are very high in vitamin C and antioxidants. These peppers can seem mild, but there's always one that's more spicy. They are roasted whole, seeds and all, and are a tasty member of the Paleo-friendly vegetable family.

Serves 4   Prep time: 15 minutes / Cook time: 30 minutes

2 tablespoons
   stone-ground mustard
2 tablespoons
   maple syrup
1 tablespoon rice vinegar
1½ teaspoons
   salt, divided
1½ teaspoons freshly
   ground black
   pepper, divided
2 cups halved radishes
1 (6-ounce bag)
   shishito peppers
1 small onion,
   thinly sliced
1½ pound pork loin filet

1. Preheat the oven to 425°F. Line a sheet pan with parchment paper. Set aside.

2. In a large bowl, whisk the mustard, maple syrup, vinegar, ½ teaspoon of salt, and ½ teaspoon of pepper to combine.

3. Add the radishes, peppers, and onion and toss to coat. Spread the vegetables on the prepared sheet pan and make room in the center for the pork loin.

4. Place the pork in the center of the vegetables. Season with the remaining 1 teaspoon of salt and 1 teaspoon of pepper.

5. Roast for 30 minutes, or until the internal temperature of pork loin reaches 145°F, or until the juices run clear.

   Option Tip: If you would like to add a little more fat and smokiness to this recipe, wrap the pork in bacon before roasting.

Per Serving
Macronutrients: 28% Fat, 48% Protein, 24% Carbs
Calories: 256; Total Fat: 8g; Saturated Fat: 2g; Protein: 31g; Total Carbs: 14g; Fiber: 3g; Net Carbs: 11g; Cholesterol: 84mg

Pork Chops with Sweet Potatoes and Brussels Sprouts

EGG-FREE, NUT-FREE

Combining Brussels sprouts and sweet potatoes creates a nutritional powerhouse. This dish is loaded with vitamin A from the sweet potatoes and vitamin C from the Brussels sprouts. When roasted, both vegetables caramelize and form a delicious combination of sweet and savory flavors.

Serves 4   **Prep time: 15 minutes / Cook time: 35 minutes**

2 tablespoons ghee

1 pound Brussels sprouts, halved lengthwise

2 sweet potatoes, peeled and chopped

1 teaspoon salt, divided

1/2 teaspoon freshly ground black pepper, divided

4 (4-ounce) pork chops

1 tablespoon chili powder

1 1/2 teaspoons ground cumin

1. Preheat the oven to 425°F. Place the ghee on the sheet pan and heat the pan in the oven until the ghee is melted and hot.

2. Toss the Brussels sprouts, sweet potatoes, 1/2 teaspoon of salt, and 1/4 teaspoon of pepper with the melted ghee, and spread to the edges of the pan.

3. Rub the pork chops all over with the chili powder, cumin, and remaining 1/2 teaspoon of salt and 1/4 teaspoon of pepper. Place the chops in the center of the sheet pan with the sweet potatoes arranged in a single layer around the pork.

4. Bake for 30 minutes, or until the internal temperature of the pork reaches 145°F, or the juices run clear and the potatoes are tender.

Option Tip: If you would like to add a bit of sweet to the heat, drizzle 1 tablespoon maple syrup over the pork chops before baking.

Per Serving

Macronutrients: 35% Fat, 31% Protein, 34% Carbs

Calories: 331; Total Fat: 13g; Saturated Fat: 7g; Protein: 26g; Total Carbs: 28g; Fiber: 7g; Net Carbs: 21g; Cholesterol: 70mg

Sheet Pan Pork Fajitas

DAIRY-FREE, EGG-FREE

This sheet pan recipe is so easy and fun to make. The fajitas are delicious with a Paleo-friendly tortilla, in a lettuce wrap, or for topping a bowl of cauliflower rice. You will need a couple small bowls in addition to the sheet pan.

Serves 4 to 6   **Prep time: 15 minutes, plus marinating time / Cook time: 15 minutes**

For the sauce

1 cup chopped fresh
  cilantro
⅓ cup extra-virgin
  olive oil
3 tablespoons
  coconut aminos
2 tablespoons freshly
  squeezed lime juice
1 jalapeño pepper,
  seeded and chopped
4 garlic cloves, minced
1 tablespoon minced
  peeled fresh ginger
1 teaspoon sesame oil

For the pork

1½ pounds boneless
  pork chops,
  thinly sliced
1 red bell pepper, sliced
1 green bell
  pepper, sliced
½ small onion, sliced
1½ teaspoons
  extra-virgin olive oil
½ teaspoon salt
Butter lettuce leaves, for
  serving (optional)

To make the sauce

In a small bowl, whisk the cilantro, olive oil, coconut aminos, lime juice, jalapeño, garlic, ginger, and sesame oil to combine. Set aside.

To make the pork

1. Place the pork in a large bowl and pour half the sauce over it. Refrigerate to marinate for 30 minutes.

2. Preheat the oven to 400°F.

3. On a sheet pan, toss together the pork, red and green bell peppers, onion, olive oil, and salt to coat.

4. Bake for 15 minutes, or until the pork is cooked through.

5. Serve with lettuce cups (if using) and the remaining sauce.

Option Tip: Many stores now offer Paleo-friendly products. Cassava and coconut flour tortillas are Paleo friendly and can be substituted for the Boston lettuce cups.

Per Serving

Macronutrients: 55% Fat, 35% Protein, 10% Carbs

Calories: 442; Total Fat: 27g; Saturated Fat: 5g; Protein: 39g; Total Carbs: 9g; Fiber: 2g; Net Carbs: 7g; Cholesterol: 112mg

Beef and Broccoli Lo Mein

DAIRY-FREE, EGG-FREE

Shirataki noodles are a low-carb noodle made from the konjac root and are a great substitute when you want the feel of an actual pasta noodle. They are toothsome and take on the flavors of the sauce they are in. They come packaged in liquid and normally have a shelf life of up to one year. Rinse the noodles well in hot water before using.

Serves 4 to 6   Prep time: 10 minutes / Cook time: 15 minutes

1½ teaspoons
   extra-virgin olive oil
12 ounces beef round
   steak, cut into
   thin strips
2 cups broccoli florets
3 scallions, white part
   only, sliced
3 garlic cloves, minced
1 cup beef broth
¼ cup coconut aminos
½ teaspoon red
   pepper flakes
1 tablespoon honey
   (optional)
2 teaspoons
   arrowroot powder
1 teaspoon sesame oil
1 (7-ounce) package
   shirataki noodles,
   rinsed in hot water
   and drained

1. Heat a large nonstick skillet over medium-high heat. Swirl in the olive oil, then add the beef. Stir-fry for 4 minutes, or until the beef is just cooked through.

2. Add the broccoli, scallions, and garlic. Stir-fry for 3 minutes, or until the broccoli has softened.

3. While the beef cooks, in a glass measuring cup, whisk the beef broth, coconut aminos, red pepper flakes, honey (if using), arrowroot powder, and sesame oil to combine. Pour the sauce over the beef and broccoli mixture and bring it to a boil. Cook, stirring constantly for 2 minutes, or until the broth begins to thicken.

4. Stir in the shirataki noodles and heat for 1 minute.

Substitution Tip: Raw zucchini noodles can be substituted for the shirataki noodles. Just stir them in as you would with the shirataki noodles in step 4.

Per Serving

Macronutrients: 32% Fat, 43% Protein, 25% Carbs

Calories: 194; Total Fat: 7g; Saturated Fat: 2g; Protein: 21g; Total Carbs: 9g; Fiber: 2g; Net Carbs: 7g; Cholesterol: 50mg

Ground Beef and Cabbage Stir-Fry

DAIRY-FREE, EGG-FREE, NUT-FREE

This skillet recipe is made to replicate the flavors of a cabbage roll, only unstuffed. You get the same delicious flavors in much less time without all the work of preparing the ingredients to make a roll. Cauliflower rice stands in for the regular rice you normally see in a cabbage roll. It may surprise you just how similar to regular rice it tastes in this recipe.

Serves 4   **Prep time: 15 minutes / Cook time: 40 minutes**

1½ teaspoons extra-virgin olive oil

½ small onion, thinly sliced

1 pound ground beef

½ head cabbage, chopped

2 cups cauliflower rice

1 (14.5-ounce) can diced tomatoes

1 tablespoon Italian seasoning

1 teaspoon salt

½ teaspoon freshly ground black pepper

1. In a large skillet over medium heat, heat the olive oil.

2. Add the onion and cook for 2 minutes, stirring occasionally.

3. Stir in the ground beef, breaking it up with a spoon, and cook for 15 minutes, or until browned.

4. Add the cabbage, cauliflower rice, tomatoes and their juices, Italian seasoning, salt, and pepper.

5. Cover the skillet and cook, stirring occasionally, for 20 minutes, or until the cabbage is tender.

Substitution Tip: If you have fresh tomatoes that need to be used, this is a great recipe to use them in! Substitute 2 large fresh tomatoes, diced, for the canned tomatoes.

Per Serving

Macronutrients: 67% Fat, 21% Protein, 12% Carbs

Calories: 431; Total Fat: 32g; Saturated Fat: 13g; Protein: 23g; Total Carbs: 13g; Fiber: 5g; Net Carbs: 8g; Cholesterol: 96mg

Thai Basil Beef

EGG-FREE

Fresh basil is good for digestion, acts as an anti-inflammatory, and helps promote a healthy gut. The flavor is strong and pungent, with a sweet smell. It is part of what makes this recipe so delicious, so be sure to pack the cup full as noted!

Serves 4 Prep time: 15 minutes / Cook time: 15 minutes

2 tablespoons
ghee, divided

1 pound skirt or sirloin
steak, thinly sliced

1 red bell pepper,
thinly sliced

1 small onion,
thinly sliced

3 garlic cloves, minced

½ cup coconut aminos

2 teaspoons fish sauce

1½ teaspoons honey

½ teaspoon salt

¼ teaspoon freshly
ground black pepper

1 cup packed fresh
basil leaves

1. In a large skillet over medium-high heat, melt 1 tablespoon of ghee.

2. Add the steak and cook for 5 minutes, stirring occasionally, until cooked through. Remove the beef from the skillet and set aside. Wipe the skillet clean with a paper towel.

3. Return the skillet to the heat and heat the remaining 1 tablespoon of ghee. Add the red bell pepper, onion, and garlic. Sauté for 5 minutes, or until the vegetables are softened.

4. Return the beef to the skillet.

5. Stir in the coconut aminos, fish sauce, honey, salt, and pepper. Bring to a boil. Reduce the heat to maintain a simmer and cook for 2 minutes.

6. Remove from the heat and stir in the fresh basil leaves before serving.

Option Tip: Serve with raw or steamed zucchini noodles or cauliflower rice.

Per Serving

Macronutrients: 39% Fat, 39% Protein, 22% Carbs

Calories: 275; Total Fat: 12g; Saturated Fat: 6g; Protein: 27g; Total Carbs: 13g; Fiber: 1g; Net Carbs: 12g; Cholesterol: 80mg

Garlic Baked Pork Chops

EGG-FREE, NUT-FREE

With super short prep time and a cook time of under 20 minutes, you will be glad to have this recipe on file. Everyone in my family raves over the results. The flavors of the ghee, garlic, and thyme infuse the pork chops for a quick but delicious meal.

Serves 2   Prep time: 5 minutes / Cook time: 20 minutes

2 (4-ounce) bone-in
   pork chops
1 teaspoon salt
½ teaspoon freshly
   ground black pepper
4 tablespoons
   ghee, divided
2 thyme sprigs
4 garlic cloves, crushed

1. Preheat the oven to 375°F.

2. Season the pork chops all over with salt and pepper. Set aside.

3. In a large skillet over medium heat, melt 2 tablespoons of ghee.

4. Add the pork chops and sear for 2 minutes per side until browned.

5. Add the remaining 2 tablespoons of ghee, the thyme, and garlic to the skillet.

6. Place the skillet in the oven and bake the pork chops for 12 minutes, or until the internal temperature reaches 145°F, or until the juices run clear.

7. Spoon the ghee from the skillet over the pork chops and serve.

   Ingredient Tip: The ghee in this recipe is very important, and I do not recommend a substitute, nor do I recommend reducing the amount used.

Per Serving

Macronutrients: 72% Fat, 23% Protein, 5% Carbs

Calories: 452; Total Fat: 36g; Saturated Fat: 21g; Protein: 26g; Total Carbs: 1g; Fiber: 0g; Net Carbs: 1g; Cholesterol: 129mg

Pork with Ginger Maple Sauce

DAIRY-FREE, EGG-FREE, NUT-FREE

This is a fall-inspired dish made with pure maple syrup and fresh ginger. Rubbed with a spice mixture of chili powder and cinnamon, these pork chops are simple to make and produce great results time after time. This is one of my favorite pork recipes, and it cooks in just about 30 minutes.

Serves 4   **Prep time: 10 minutes / Cook time: 35 minutes**

4 teaspoons extra-virgin olive oil, divided
1 onion, chopped
1 tablespoon minced peeled fresh ginger
1 teaspoon chili powder
½ teaspoon salt
½ teaspoon freshly ground black pepper
½ teaspoon ground cinnamon
4 (4-ounce) bone-in pork chops
½ cup chicken broth
¼ cup maple syrup

1. In a large skillet over medium-low heat, heat 2 teaspoons of olive oil. Add the onion and sauté for 10 minutes, or until golden brown and tender. Add the ginger and cook, stirring, for 2 minutes more. Remove from the skillet and set aside.

2. In a small bowl, whisk the chili powder, salt, pepper, and cinnamon to combine. Rub the spices over both sides of the pork chops.

3. Place the skillet over medium heat and add the remaining 2 teaspoons of oil to heat. Add the chops and cook for 3 minutes per side until browned.

4. Add the chicken broth, maple syrup, and onion mixture to the skillet. Bring to a boil, then reduce the heat to maintain a simmer. Cover the skillet and cook for 8 minutes, or until the meat is tender. Remove the pork from the skillet and keep warm.

5. Bring the broth mixture to a boil. Cook, uncovered, for 2 minutes, or until the liquid is thickened and reduced to about ½ cup. Serve the chops with the sauce.

Substitution Tip: The carbs in this dish are a little on the high side from the maple syrup. If you would like to reduce the carbs, use a sugar-free maple syrup in its place.

Per Serving

Macronutrients: 42% Fat, 30% Protein, 28% Carbs

Calories: 278; Total Fat: 13g; Saturated Fat: 4g; Protein: 21g; Total Carbs: 17g; Fiber: 1g; Net Carbs: 16g; Cholesterol: 61mg

Taco-Seasoned Pork Chops

DAIRY-FREE, EGG-FREE, NUT-FREE

Do you go bone in or boneless with a pork chop? For me, it depends on how many other ingredients are involved and how long the cook time needs to be. I use thinner-cut boneless pork chops for this recipe. Thinner chops cook faster and remain juicy with the combination of a short cooking time and the sauce.

Serves 6   **Prep time: 10 minutes / Cook time: 10 minutes**

1 tablespoon extra-virgin
   olive oil
6 (4-ounce) thin-cut
   boneless pork
   loin chops
1 (8-ounce) can
   tomato sauce
1 cup water
1 small onion, sliced
1 tablespoon chili powder
1½ teaspoons
   ground cumin
1 teaspoon paprika
½ teaspoon
   garlic powder
½ teaspoon
   dried oregano
½ teaspoon salt
¼ teaspoon freshly
   ground black pepper
Chopped fresh cilantro,
   for garnish (optional)

1. In a large skillet over medium heat, heat the olive oil.

2. Add the pork chops and cook for 3 minutes per side, or until lightly browned.

3. In a small bowl, whisk the tomato sauce, 1 cup water, onion, chili powder, cumin, paprika, garlic powder, oregano, salt, and pepper to combine. Pour the sauce over the pork and bring the mixture to a boil. Cook for 2 minutes, or until the sauce has thickened.

4. Garnish with cilantro (if using) and serve.

Option Tip: I love to make my own guacamole to serve with this recipe. Just mash 1 avocado with ½ cup of Paleo-approved salsa for a fast and simple side.

Per Serving

Macronutrients: 36% Fat, 59% Protein, 5% Carbs

Calories: 185; Total Fat: 8g; Saturated Fat: 2g; Protein: 22g; Total Carbs: 6g; Fiber: 2g; Net Carbs: 4g; Cholesterol: 55mg

Glazed Pork Chops with Brussels Sprouts

EGG-FREE, NUT-FREE

As the maple glaze on these pork chops heats up, it produces a caramelized flavor on the Brussels sprouts as they roast. Be sure to stir the Brussels sprouts after 10 minutes of cooking so they brown evenly.

Serves 4 Prep time: 10 minutes / Cook time: 20 minutes

2 tablespoons ghee

¼ cup maple syrup

½ teaspoon cayenne pepper

½ teaspoon garlic powder

½ teaspoon smoked paprika

½ teaspoon salt, plus more for seasoning

¼ teaspoon freshly ground black pepper, plus more for seasoning

4 thick-cut boneless pork chops

1 pound Brussels sprouts, halved lengthwise

1. Preheat the oven to 350°F. Place the ghee on a sheet pan and place it in the oven while it preheats to melt.

2. In a small bowl, whisk the maple syrup, cayenne, garlic powder, paprika, salt, and black pepper to combine.

3. Lay the pork chops in the center of the sheet pan. Brush the maple mixture over the pork chops, covering them completely.

4. Arrange the Brussels sprouts around the pork chops and lightly season with salt and pepper, if desired.

5. Roast the pork and Brussels sprouts for 10 minutes.

6. Take the pan out of the oven and stir the sprouts. Roast for 10 minutes more, or until the internal temperature of the pork reaches 145°F, or until the juices run clear.

Substitution Tip: If the carbs are too high for you in this recipe, use a sugar-free maple syrup in place of the pure maple syrup to reduce the carb intake to 6 net carbs.

Per Serving

Macronutrients: 38% Fat, 33% Protein, 29% Carbs

Calories: 307; Total Fat: 13g; Saturated Fat: 7g; Protein: 25g; Total Carbs: 24g; Fiber: 5g; Net Carbs: 19g; Cholesterol: 60mg

Pork Chops with Apples and Onions

DAIRY-FREE, EGG-FREE

This recipe is a great dish to serve in the fall when apples are in season. I choose Honeycrisp apples because of their crisp, sweet, juicy bite. They stay firm while cooking and the result is an apple you can still stick your fork into. Apples pair deliciously with the onion cream sauce and pork chops. Serve with Stuffed Acorn Squash (page 87), if desired.

Serves 4   Prep time: 10 minutes / Cook time: 20 minutes

4 (6-ounce) bone-in
  pork chops
½ teaspoon salt
¼ teaspoon freshly
  ground black pepper
3 teaspoons extra-virgin
  olive oil, divided
2 Honeycrisp apples,
  cut into ½-inch-
  thick wedges
1 small red onion,
  thinly sliced
1 tablespoon chopped
  fresh sage
1½ teaspoons chopped
  fresh rosemary
⅓ cup chicken broth
½ cup coconut cream
¼ cup Dijon mustard

1. Season both sides of the pork chops with salt and pepper.

2. In a large skillet over medium-high heat, heat 1½ teaspoons of olive oil.

3. Add the pork chops to the skillet and sear for 3 minutes per side. Transfer the pork chops to a plate and set aside.

4. Add the remaining 1½ teaspoons of olive oil to the skillet along with the apple slices and red onion. Season with sage and rosemary. Sauté for 4 minutes, or until the onion is translucent and the apples are still firm. Transfer to a plate and set aside.

5. Return the skillet to the heat and add the chicken broth, coconut cream, and Dijon mustard. Whisk to combine. Bring the sauce to a boil, then reduce the heat to maintain a simmer. Cook for 3 minutes.

6. Add the pork chops, apples, and onions back to the skillet. Simmer in the sauce for 4 minutes, or until the pork chops are cooked through and the sauce has reduced by half.

Substitution Tip: If Honeycrisp apples are not available, find an apple that is firm and holds up well to cooking. The best substitute would be the Cortland or Braeburn apple.

Per Serving

Macronutrients: 49% Fat, 32% Protein, 19% Carbs

Calories: 445; Total Fat: 24g; Saturated Fat: 10g; Protein: 36g; Total Carbs: 14g; Fiber: 3g; Net Carbs: 11g; Cholesterol: 104mg

Beef-Stuffed Peppers

DAIRY-FREE, EGG-FREE, NUT-FREE

I use red bell peppers for this recipe, because green bell peppers have a bitter taste, despite the fact they are called a sweet pepper. Red bell peppers get that sweetness from being on the vine longer. The sweet contrast goes well with the beef and sausage filling.

Serves 6   Prep time: 15 minutes / Cook time: 40 minutes

1 pound ground beef

8 ounces ground sausage

1 (14-ounce) can diced tomatoes, drained

1 (8-ounce) can tomato sauce

1 cup cooked cauliflower rice

2 garlic cloves, minced

2 tablespoons nutritional yeast flakes

1 tablespoon Italian seasoning

1 teaspoon salt

½ teaspoon freshly ground black pepper

½ teaspoon red pepper flakes

6 red bell peppers, halved and seeded

Minced fresh parsley, for garnish (optional)

1. Preheat the oven to 350°F.

2. In a large bowl, combine the ground beef, ground sausage, tomatoes, tomato sauce, cauliflower rice, garlic, nutritional yeast flakes, Italian seasoning, salt, pepper, and red pepper flakes.

3. Mix well. Evenly fill each pepper half with the meat mixture. Place the filled peppers on a sheet pan.

4. Bake for 40 minutes, or until the meat is cooked through.

5. Garnish with fresh parsley (if using).

Ingredient Tip: Nutritional yeast flakes are used for the cheesy flavor they impart. If you don't have any on hand, leave them out and there is no need to substitute another ingredient.

Per Serving
Macronutrients: 62% Fat, 22% Protein, 16% Carbs
Calories: 421; Total Fat: 29g; Saturated Fat: 11g; Protein: 23g; Total Carbs: 16g; Fiber: 4g; Net Carbs: 12g; Cholesterol: 91mg

Hamburger Steaks Stroganoff

EGG-FREE

These hamburger steaks are delicious next to a side of mashed cauliflower. Steam a small head of cauliflower until tender, then blend it in a food processor with 4 tablespoons melted ghee plus salt and pepper to taste.

Serves 4   Prep time: 15 minutes / Cook time: 20 minutes

1 pound ground beef

2 teaspoons coconut aminos

¾ teaspoon salt, divided

¾ teaspoon freshly ground black pepper, divided

3 teaspoons ghee, divided

8 ounces baby portobello mushrooms, halved

¼ cup chopped onion

¼ cup beef broth

¼ cup dry red wine

2 teaspoons arrowroot powder

1. In a large bowl, combine the ground beef, coconut aminos, ½ teaspoon of salt, and ½ teaspoon of pepper. Divide the meat mixture into 4 portions, shaping each into a patty.

2. In a large skillet over medium-high heat, melt 1½ teaspoons of ghee. Add the beef patties and cook for 3 minutes per side. Remove from the skillet and set aside.

3. Melt the remaining 1½ teaspoons of ghee in the skillet. Stir in the mushrooms and onion. Cook for 5 minutes, stirring frequently.

4. In a small bowl, whisk the beef broth, red wine, and arrowroot powder. Pour the broth into the hot skillet and cook for 1 minute, until thickened and slightly reduced, stirring frequently.

5. Move the mushroom-onion mixture to the side and return the beef patties to the skillet. Cover and cook for 5 minutes, or until the beef is cooked through.

Substitution Tip: The red wine is used in this recipe for flavor. If you prefer, eliminate the wine and increase the beef broth to ½ cup.

Per Serving
Macronutrients: 73% Fat, 20% Protein, 7% Carbs
Calories: 420; Total Fat: 34g; Saturated Fat: 15g; Protein: 21g; Total Carbs: 5g; Fiber: 1g; Net Carbs: 4g; Cholesterol: 104mg

Roast Beef and Sweet Potatoes

DAIRY-FREE, EGG-FREE, NUT-FREE

The cinnamon in this recipe does more than add sweet warmth. It's loaded with antioxidants, has anti-inflammatory properties, and may cut the risk of heart disease. It also lowers blood sugar levels and can have an antidiabetic effect.

Serves 8   **Prep time: 15 minutes / Cook time: 1 hour, 30 minutes**

1 tablespoon extra-virgin olive oil

1 (3-pound) boneless beef roast

1 tablespoon chili powder

1 teaspoon ground cinnamon

1 teaspoon salt

½ teaspoon freshly ground black pepper

2 large sweet potatoes, chopped

4 large carrots, quartered

1 small onion, chopped

¾ cup beef broth, divided

2 teaspoons arrowroot powder (optional)

1. Select Sauté on the Instant Pot and add the olive oil to heat. Add the roast and sear for 2 minutes per side, or until browned. Sprinkle with the chili powder, cinnamon, salt, and pepper.

2. Arrange the sweet potatoes, carrots, and onion around the roast. Pour ½ cup of beef broth over the roast.

3. Lock the lid into place and seal the vent. Select Manual and cook on High Pressure for 1 hour.

4. After cooking, let the pressure release naturally for 10 minutes, then quick release any remaining pressure. Carefully unlock and remove the lid. Remove the roast from the Instant Pot and set aside.

5. To make gravy, if desired, skim the broth to remove any bits left in the pot. In a small bowl, whisk the arrowroot (if using) and remaining ¼ cup of beef broth until dissolved. Select Sauté and bring the broth in the pot to a boil. Whisk in the arrowroot mixture and cook for 2 minutes, or until the broth has thickened.

Ingredient Tip: If you love a little sweetness added to your food, drizzle 1 tablespoon of honey over the roast and vegetables after the beef broth has been added to the pot in step 2.

Slow Cooker Tip: To make this in a slow cooker, it's as easy as placing the roast in the bottom of the crock, sprinkling it with the seasonings, arranging the vegetables around the roast, and covering and cooking on high heat for 6 hours or on low heat for 8 hours.

Per Serving

Macronutrients: 34% Fat, 49% Protein, 17% Carbs

Calories: 374; Total Fat: 14g; Saturated Fat: 4g; Protein: 46g; Total Carbs: 14g; Fiber: 3g; Net Carbs: 11g; Cholesterol: 121mg

Instant Pot Pork Ribs

DAIRY-FREE, EGG-FREE, NUT-FREE

Get ready for tender meat that literally falls off the bone! The Instant Pot cooks these ribs so quickly and makes them so tender, you won't believe how easy they are to make. Cooked under pressure, these ribs will be ready and on the table in less than 1 hour. You will need a 6-quart or larger Instant Pot for this recipe.

Serves 8 **Prep time: 10 minutes / Cook time: 30 minutes**

1 rack baby back pork ribs, with membrane removed from the back of the ribs

2 tablespoons paprika

1 tablespoon garlic powder

1 tablespoon onion powder

1 tablespoon ground chipotle pepper

1½ teaspoons ground cumin

1 tablespoon sea salt

1 cup beef broth

1. Place the ribs on a clean cutting board. Evenly sprinkle the paprika, garlic powder, onion powder, chipotle pepper, cumin, and salt over the front and back of the ribs. Rub the dry spices over the ribs, covering them completely.

2. Pour the beef broth into the Instant Pot, then place a rack inside the pot. Place the ribs on the rack, standing up on their short side and wrapping around the inside of the pot.

3. Lock the lid into place and seal the vent. Select Manual and cook on High Pressure for 30 minutes.

4. After cooking, let the pressure release naturally for 15 minutes, then quick release any remaining pressure. Carefully unlock and remove the lid.

Option Tip: These ribs will already have a lot of flavor from the dry rub. However, if you like sauce with your ribs, serve them with a Paleo barbecue sauce on the side for dipping. Or, take it a step further: Brush the cooked ribs with barbecue sauce and place them on a baking sheet under the broiler for 5 minutes to brown.

Slow Cooker Tip: Follow the instructions for seasoning the ribs in step 1. Add the beef broth to the slow cooker and place the ribs, bone-side down, in the crock. Cover the cooker and cook on low heat for 8 hours, or until the meat easily falls away from the bone.

Per Serving

Macronutrients: 71% Fat, 22% Protein, 7% Carbs

Calories: 253; Total Fat: 20g; Saturated Fat: 8g; Protein: 14g; Total Carbs: 2g; Fiber: 1g; Net Carbs: 1g; Cholesterol: 68mg

Smothered Pork Chops

EGG-FREE

This delicious recipe was easy to convert to dairy-free, and by using ghee and almond milk, I was able to retain the flavor and feel of a creamy milk gravy.

Serves 4   Prep time: 10 minutes / Cook time: 40 minutes

1 teaspoon garlic powder

1 teaspoon salt, divided

½ teaspoon freshly ground black pepper, divided

4 (4-ounce) pork chops

2 tablespoons ghee, divided

1 small onion, sliced

1½ cups chicken broth

¼ cup almond milk

2 teaspoons arrowroot powder

1. Sprinkle the garlic powder, ½ teaspoon of salt, and ¼ teaspoon of pepper over the pork chops on both sides.

2. In a large skillet over medium-high heat, melt 1 tablespoon of ghee. Place the pork chops in the skillet and cook for 5 minutes per side until well browned. Transfer to a plate and set aside.

3. Melt the remaining 1 tablespoon of ghee in the skillet. Reduce the heat to medium and add the onion, remaining ½ teaspoon of salt, and ¼ teaspoon of pepper. Cook the onion for 15 minutes, stirring occasionally, or until the onion is caramelized.

4. In a large glass measuring cup, whisk the chicken broth, almond milk, and arrowroot powder. Add the sauce to the skillet and bring to a boil.

5. Return the pork chops to the skillet and reduce the heat to low. Simmer for 10 minutes, or until the pork chops reach an internal temperature of 145°F.

Substitution Tip: If desired, substitute coconut milk for the almond milk. The flavor profile will change slightly, but the recipe will still be delicious.

Per Serving
Macronutrients: 49% Fat, 44% Protein, 7% Carbs
Calories: 255; Total Fat: 14g; Saturated Fat: 7g; Protein: 28g; Total Carbs: 4g; Fiber: 0g; Net Carbs: 4g; Cholesterol: 72mg

Slow Cooker Meatballs

DAIRY-FREE

My family loves this slow cooker recipe. It is as easy as placing the raw meatballs in the bottom of the slow cooker and covering them with a sauce to simmer for hours! When it is time for dinner, I like to steam 4 cups of zucchini noodles in my microwave steamer for just 1 minute, then serve the meatballs and sauce over the noodles.

Serves 8   **Prep time: 15 minutes / Cook time: 6 hours**

For the meatballs

1½ pounds ground beef
1 large egg
½ cup almond meal
1 teaspoon salt
1 teaspoon onion powder
½ teaspoon
garlic powder

For the sauce

1 (28-ounce) can crushed
tomatoes
1 (14-ounce) can diced
tomatoes
½ cup water
½ cup chopped onion
3 garlic cloves, minced
1 tablespoon Italian
seasoning
½ teaspoon salt
¼ teaspoon freshly
ground black pepper
1 (6-ounce) can
tomato paste

To make the meatballs

In a large bowl, combine the ground beef, egg, almond meal, salt, onion powder, and garlic powder. Mix well. Shape the meat mixture into 2-inch meatballs and place them in the slow cooker.

To make the sauce

1. To the slow cooker, add the crushed tomatoes, diced tomatoes and their juices, ½ cup water, onion, garlic, Italian seasoning, salt, and pepper. Gently stir to combine.

2. Cover the cooker and cook on low heat for 5 hours.

3. Stir in the tomato paste. Adjust the heat to high and cook, uncovered, for 1 hour.

Substitution Tip: Make this recipe nut-free by substituting ½ cup ground pork rinds for the almond meal.

Instant Pot Tip: Select the Sauté setting and add 1 tablespoon of olive oil to heat. Working in two batches, add the meatballs and brown on all sides. Once all the meatballs are browned, add all the ingredients in step 1 (to make the sauce) and the tomato paste to the Instant Pot. Lock the lid in place and seal the vent. Select Manual and cook on High Pressure for 7 minutes. After cooking, let the pressure release naturally for 5 minutes, then quick release any remaining pressure.

Per Serving
Macronutrients: 59% Fat, 24% Protein, 17% Carbs
Calories: 335; Total Fat: 22g; Saturated Fat: 8g; Protein: 20g; Total Carbs: 14g; Fiber: 4g; Net Carbs: 10g; Cholesterol: 87mg

Pot Roast Dinner

EGG-FREE, NUT-FREE

Turnips are a great choice to substitute for potatoes, especially when making a pot roast dinner. Here, the turnips are cooked in the broth, absorbing the flavor of the beef similar to the way potatoes do. Since I have been making this recipe, my husband brags to everyone how great turnips are as a potato substitute.

Serves 10   **Prep time: 15 minutes / Cook time: 5 hours, 30 minutes**

1 tablespoon ghee
1 (4-pound) boneless
   chuck roast
1½ teaspoons salt
¾ teaspoon freshly
   ground black pepper
4 cups beef broth
2 tablespoons
   tomato paste
2 cups chopped
   peeled turnip
1 large onion, quartered
4 large carrots,
   quartered
4 garlic cloves, minced
2 rosemary sprigs
2 thyme sprigs
¼ cup water
2 teaspoons
   arrowroot powder

1. Preheat the oven to 325°F.

2. In a large Dutch oven over medium-high heat, melt the ghee.

3. Season the roast on all sides with the salt and pepper. Place the roast in the Dutch oven and sear for 4 minutes per side until browned. Transfer the roast to a plate.

4. In the Dutch oven, whisk the beef broth and tomato paste to combine.

5. Return the beef to the Dutch oven and arrange the turnip, onion, carrots, garlic, rosemary, and thyme around the beef. Cover the pot and transfer to the oven.

6. Roast for 5 hours.

7. Remove the roast from the oven and transfer the meat and vegetables to a serving platter. Set aside and keep warm.

8. Strain the beef broth from the pot using a fine-mesh sieve set over a bowl. Discard any solids and the herbs. Return the broth to the Dutch oven, place it over medium-high heat, and bring to a boil.

9. In a small bowl, whisk ¼ cup water and the arrowroot powder until dissolved. Whisk the arrowroot mixture into the boiling broth. Cook for 2 minutes, whisking constantly, or until the gravy begins to thicken. Serve the roast and vegetables with the gravy.

Leftovers Tip: This is a large-batch recipe that is perfect for Sunday dinner with the whole family. Leftovers are just as delicious rewarmed or made into hash for breakfast the next day.

Per Serving

Macronutrients: 37% Fat, 53% Protein, 10% Carbs

Calories: 368; Total Fat: 15; Saturated Fat: 5g; Protein: 49g; Total Carbs: 8g; Fiber: 2g; Net Carbs: 6g; Cholesterol: 133mg

Sweet-and-Sour Meat Loaf

DAIRY-FREE, NUT-FREE

Ground pork rinds have become a very popular low-carb substitute for bread crumbs. You can buy them pre-ground, or buy the rinds themselves and grind them in a food processor, storing what you don't use in this recipe in an airtight container in your pantry.

Serves 8   **Prep time: 15 minutes / Cook time: 5 hours**

For the meatloaf

Olive oil
1 pound ground beef
¼ cup finely
   chopped onion
½ green bell
   pepper, chopped
½ cup ground pork rinds
1 large egg
1½ teaspoons Italian
   seasoning
½ teaspoon salt
½ teaspoon freshly
   ground black pepper

For the topping

3 tablespoons
   sugar-free ketchup
1 tablespoon honey
1 tablespoon vinegar
2 bay leaves

To make the meatloaf

1. Lightly coat the bottom of a slow cooker crock with olive oil.

2. In a large bowl, combine the ground beef, onion, green bell pepper, pork rinds, egg, Italian seasoning, salt, and pepper. Mix with your hands to combine well, then shape the meat mixture into a loaf and place it in the slow cooker.

To make the topping

1. In a small bowl, whisk the ketchup, honey, and vinegar to blend. Spoon the sauce over the meatloaf. Top with the bay leaves.

2. Cover the cooker and cook on low heat for 5 hours, or until the internal temperature is at 160°F and the loaf is cooked through. Slice and serve.

Cooking Tip: If you prefer, mix the meatloaf and place it in a loaf pan, top with the sauce, and bake at 350°F for 40 minutes, or until the internal temperature reaches 160°F.

Instant Pot Tip: Line the inner pot with a 12-inch-square piece of aluminum foil. Mix and form the meatloaf, then place it in the Instant Pot and cover with the sauce. Lock the lid in place and seal the vent. Select Manual and cook on High Pressure for 30 minutes. After cooking, let the pressure release naturally for 10 minutes, then quick release any remaining pressure. Carefully lift the foil from the Instant Pot and transfer the meatloaf to a serving platter.

Per Serving

Macronutrients: 69% Fat, 23% Protein, 8% Carbs

Calories: 210; Total Fat: 16g; Saturated Fat: 7g; Protein: 12g; Total Carbs: 4g; Fiber: 0g; Net Carbs: 4g; Cholesterol: 73mg

MEASUREMENT CONVERSIONS

VOLUME EQUIVALENTS (LIQUID)

US Standard (ounces)	US Standard (approximate)	Metric
2 tablespoons	1 fl.oz.	30 mL
¼ cup	2 fl. oz.	60 mL
½ cup	4 fl. oz.	120 mL
1 cup	8 fl. oz.	240 mL
1½ cups	12 fl.oz.	355 mL
2 cups or 1 pint	16 fl. oz.	475 mL
4 cups or 1 quart	32 fl. oz.	1 L
1 gallon	128 fl.oz.	4 L

OVEN TEMPERATURES

Fahrenheit (F)	Celsius (C) (approximate)
250°F	120°C
300°F	150°C
325°F	165°C
350°F	180°C
375°F	190°C
400°F	200°C
425°F	220°C
450°F	230°C

VOLUME EQUIVALENTS (DRY)

US Standard	Metric (approximate)
⅛ teaspoon	0.5 mL
¼ teaspoon	1 mL
½ teaspoon	2 mL
¾ teaspoon	4 mL
1 teaspoon	5 mL
1 tablespoon	15 mL
¼ cup	59 mL
⅓ cup	79 mL
½ cup	118 mL
⅔ cup	156 mL
¾ cup	177 mL
1 cup	235 mL
2 cups or 1 pint	475 mL
3 cups	700 mL
4 cups or 1 quart	1 L

WEIGHT EQUIVALENTS

US Standard	Metric (approximate)
½ ounce	15 g
1 ounce	30 g
2 ounces	60 g
4 ounces	115 g
8 ounces	225 g
12 ounces	340 g
16 ounces or 1 pound	455 g

INDEX

ACKNOWLEDGMENTS

I would like to thank my husband, Phillip, and children Justin, Christopher, and Miriah for their encouragement and for believing I could accomplish anything if I tried. I also would like to thank my friend Kristin, who has been there for me every step of my career as a blogger over the last two years.

ABOUT THE AUTHOR

 **Shelby Law Ruttan** was brought up in a very close-knit family where traditions were the center of the home. Family dinners were important, and everyone would gather for special occasions, bringing the best recipes each person had to offer. She carries on those traditions with her own family and puts them in writing via her websites, Grumpy's Honeybunch and Honeybunch Hunts, to share with others, focusing on the lifestyle and food she feeds her family.

CPSIA information can be obtained
at www.ICGtesting.com
Printed in the USA
LVHW011603110320
649595LV00001BA/1